A BRIDGE NAMED Susan

A BRIDGE NAMED
Susan

SHARON CHASE HOSELEY

Library of Congress Control Number:		2017903598
ISBN:	Hardcover	978-1-5245-8993-6
	Softcover	978-1-5245-8992-9
	eBook	978-1-5245-9033-8

Print information available on the last page.

Rev. date: 03/08/2017

To order additional copies of this book, contact:
Xlibris
1-888-795-4274
www.Xlibris.com
Orders@Xlibris.com
756224

CONTENTS

Prologue

It was fortunate Idaho began recording reports of "live" births in 1905. It was difficult for some people my age to prove they existed. To qualify for a birth certificate, I had to send an application to the capital in Boise, along with my baptismal certificate and two handwritten statements from people who were present at my birth. A large brown envelope arrived two months later. I eagerly tore it open and read the beautifully handwritten Certificate of Birth:

Name, Susan Kole
Date of Birth, June 30, 1910
Place of Birth, Gifford, Idaho
Mother, Musetta Zelma Denny Kole Father, John Kole
Delivered by Maria Kole, midwife, mother of John Kole.

What a shock! I believed I was born on the Kole homestead in Reubens, Idaho.

The homestead was eleven miles from Reubens and eight miles from Gifford. Gifford won my birthplace by closest proximity. At the age of thirty, I still struggle with my place in life, where I'm from and where I belong.

I live on the edge, searching for the real me, trying to prove I'm important and worthy to be loved. I've silently watched and learned from a distant mother, a cruel brother, and a silent husband. My observations have produced a strong determination to span to the next generation a tranquil life, filled with love and acceptance. God is the foundation as I build my life bridge, the bridge named Susan.

The Foundation

Do good, be rich in good works, be generous
and ready to share, thus storing up treasure for yourselves as a
good foundation for the future, so that they may
take hold of that which is truly life.
—I Timothy 6:19

Dedication

To Susan, a great storyteller who transported people, places, and events into reality, framing a bridge of love to me, the next generation.

FARM HOUSE of

John & Minnie Kole & Family

Chapter 1

Devastated

"Stand still," Mama commanded as she jerked the hairbrush out of my hand and pulled hard through my tangled mop. Instinctively, I screamed. "You will not scream at me," she threatened. She shoved me down on the stool in front of the kitchen wash basin where I'd been standing on my tippy-toes, trying to see in our cracked mirror.

I jammed my fist in my mouth and shut my eyes tight, trying to concentrate on the safe place in my mind where I ran through fields of yellow daisies on a warm day.

Tears ran down my cheeks as she again and again attacked the knots of hair. I was shaking with fright at my mama's anger. I had crossed the line into being a bad girl. I could never do enough to please my mama. Getting rats' nests out of long natural curls was impossible for this five-year-old. I tried. Oh, how I tried, but the more I tried, the worse it tangled.

"You're not going anywhere looking like this!" Mama yelled. "Why can't you do anything for yourself? I've got more important things to do than comb your hair."

The brush hit the floor, and a drawer opened. "I'll take care of this problem right now. You annoy me to no end, child . . . nothing but a constant pain in my side," Mama snapped. I felt her strong working hands gather my curls to the back of my neck. She yanked hard. My eyes flew open and caught a glance of silver scissors in the mirror.

I choked out, "No!" A grinding sound vibrated through my entire body as she chomped away. "Please, Mama. Not my curls. I love my curls." I was horrified.

My mind flew to Grandpa Kole's words. "I love your beautiful black curls, little black-eyed Susan. I'm lucky to have such a gorgeous little granddaughter." Could he ever stand the sight of me again? Boys have short hair. Girls don't.

She chewed away with the dull scissors that had opened feed sacks, cut paper, string, flowers, and cloth, until each ringlet fell to the floor. Fearful of being poked or losing an ear, I could feel my body turned to stone.

A grating snip lobbed off another chunk. I let out a screech.

"Quiet!" Mama demanded as she kept whacking. "At five years old, you should be able to take care of yourself. Never saw such a slow girl in all my days."

I pushed my sobs deep inside, feeling uglier with each cut.

Suddenly, the snipping stopped, the drawer opened, the scissors clanked in, and Mama's footsteps stomped out the kitchen door.

I opened my eyes. Piles of black curls lay heaped on the floor. Sobs burst from my throat. I fell to my knees and buried my face deep in the ringlets that were no longer a part of me. They represented my ache for Mama's love. I tucked two in my apron pocket for a keepsake, then swept up the rest, trying to please Mama.

I didn't leave the house or the farm. How could I? I was the homeliest creature on earth. What would I tell people when they raised their eyebrows and joked about my hair getting caught in the thresher? I was ugly, ugly, ugly. Our farm, miles from anyone, gave me a safe sanctuary to hide under my wide-brimmed sun hat while working in the garden. I prayed God would grow my hair out before I started my first year of school in October.

In August, Mama handed me a bucket. "Get water from the pond and water the garden," she commanded. "Can't have wilted plants. Everything will be too tough to eat." It was all I could do to carry a half bucket, and our garden was big. Dipper after dipper, I watered each plant.

I sat by the pond to rest. A movement in the tall grass caught my eye. *What's that?* I stared at the spot. The plants shook again. I crept closer. A little green frog leaped away and splatted into the pond. I laughed. He crawled onto a blade of grass hanging over the water and sat blinking his big eyes at me. "Hello, little fellow," I whispered. "Are you going to be my friend?" He answered with one croak and plopped back into the water. I smiled and continued my job.

Day after day, Froggy met me at the pond as I carted water. Closer and closer he moved to my still hand I reached toward him. One day he hopped onto my hand and stared at me with unblinking eyes. I was giggling inside. I had become the friend of a frog.

My hand was like the bridge Papa built over the creek to push the wheelbarrow of potatoes from the patch to the cellar. It was a safe way for Froggy to get from his water home to me, his new friend.

Ah, this is what I want with Mama, I thought, *a bridge between us. I want her to love me, to gently touch me, to smile at me, to talk to me. Her face holds smiles and laughter for others, but not for me.*

With deep creases between her eyes, Mama addressed me with a downturned mouth. "Susan, you mustn't do that. Good girls don't do things like that." I never understood what good girls do and don't do, since that would be the end of the discussion.

I tried hard to please, to be a good girl. My heart needed her words of thanks that would build a bridge between us or for her simply to say, "I love you."

Chapter 2

Feed the Chickens

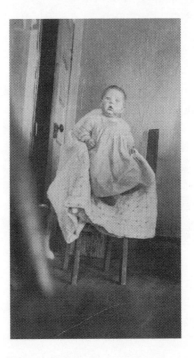

The haircut wasn't the first time I felt my mother's anger and resentment. Papa told me stories of when I was a toddler, but my first strong memory was the job of feeding the chickens.

I entered the world as a farm child on June 30, 1910. It was time for planting in the hills of Idaho, where snows melt late. Orders came from the midwife for Mama: stay in bed four weeks, lift nothing, no steps to be taken, except for a quick use of the chamber pot; sit up only to eat, followed by at least an hour's sleep.

Mama's sisters took turns coming to the house to plant the garden and get meals. Papa told me later I was colicky. My uncontrollable cries demanded too much from a woman of thirty-seven. People waiting on her and caring for her husband and three-year-old son was humiliating. Independence, pride, and responsibility formed her core character. At the age of eight, she had endured a nine-month wagon-train trip with her homesteading parents and younger sisters. Her demanding father never allowed complaining or laziness.

On top of the inconvenience, frustration, and worry about getting seeds into the ground for winter's food supply, I was a girl. "A girl's no good at running a farm," she told Papa. "I'll see she's fed, dry, and warm enough, but that's it." As far as Mama was concerned, I was to be invisible; tolerated only as long as I did what I was told.

I learned quickly to abide by that rule. By the time I was five, I scrubbed clothes on the washboard, swept and hand-scrubbed wooden floors spotless, weeded rows of baby radishes, and fed the chickens. I gathered eggs, picked berries, dried dishes, set the table for dinner and supper, and made the beds. Mama kept me busy from the time I got up until bedtime. I was a good girl, always trying to do what was asked, but not earning recognition from my mama. More than once, the hairbrush that I couldn't get to tame my curls became the consequences for some task I couldn't accomplish to Mama's expectations. What more could I do to please her?

It seemed to me Mama had too high expectations of me and no expectations for my brother, Johnny, who was three years older. I was given jobs with no directions and learned by failing. Johnny, on the other hand, did very little. When he went to the fields to work with Papa, he would simply quit and go to the house. No one dared make him do anything. I was jealous.

My first real job assignment was feeding the chickens. We only fed them in the evening after a free-run-of-the-farm day. Farm chickens have three jobs: eating bugs and weed seeds, laying eggs, and providing chicken dinner. At my young age, I didn't understand why they lived with us. I only knew they were noisy, smelly, and sometimes downright scary.

Right after my third birthday, Mama gave me a small pail half full of chicken feed. "Here," she said. "It's time for you to start earning your keep around here. You're gonna feed the chickens."

I'm sure my dark brown eyes grew as big as the saucers Papa drank his coffee from. Fear gripped me down to my little bare toes. I didn't dare say a word. My mama had said it, and I'd do it. I'd prove to her that I was a big girl. Then she'd love me. I took a deep breath and headed toward the open chicken-pen door. I had watched Mama feed the chickens. She'd call, "Here, chick, chick, chick." The chickens would come running, knowing sweet wheat or oats waited as dessert after their day's feast of seeds and bugs. It was also the way to get all of them into the pen. Mama locked the door after the feeding, so they were safe from fox and coyotes at night.

My three-year-old mind kept repeating over and over. "Go feed chicks, go feed chicks." I was now inside the pen. One old red hen spied me and started running toward the gate. "Chick, chick . . ." I began. I was swiftly surrounded by hens and one white rooster nearly as tall as me. They were demanding; not a bit polite. They screeched and squawked and stuck their heads in my little bucket, fighting for a more than their fair share. When they started pecking me, my brave face dissolved into tears and terrified screams. Surrounded by beaks, feathered wing-beaters and long sharp toenails, I was trapped. I dropped the bucket and fell to my knees, curling up into a ball with my hands over my head while the chickens fought over the wheat spilling from the can.

Wailing as only a three-year-old can, I felt a pair of large hands go around my middle and lift me from the dirt into strong, safe arms. My papa had rescued me. My hero! I snuggled my face into his broad shoulder and clasped my arms around his neck as he carried me through the gate and locked it. My sobs came slower as he carried me to the house. I heard my mama and Johnny laughing. *Well, I didn't think it was funny!* Papa sat in the old porch rocking chair, quietly singing and humming, and held me close until my last tear fell. The vibration of his voice lulled me to sleep.

I had failed at my first job.

Chapter 3

Painting the Barn

John Kale and daughter Susan

My favorite jobs were in the fields with Papa: picking up rocks the plow turned over, riding Old Bess out to fix the fence, and running the seed spreader. Mama allowed me to go if I had my other work done. Papa was kind, gentle, hummed to himself, and had a hearty little chuckle.

One day late in June, right before my sixth birthday, he woke me early. "Susan," he whispered, "I've got a special job for you today."

"Hmmm?" I murmured my sleepy question.

"Get dressed in house clothes and meet me at the barn," he whispered again and left to wake Johnny.

It was getting daylight when we stumbled to the barn. Papa was waiting for us. He covered our clothes with old gunny sacks and gave both of us a small bucket of red paint. "We get to paint the barn," he announced with a wide smile on his face. "The first four boards 'round the bottom of the barn are yours, Susan." He handed me a brush. "Johnny, now that you're nine, you're tall enough to do the next four. I'll do the rest. Don't want you kids on the ladder."

The snow had melted; it hadn't rained for several weeks. "The boards are dry enough to hold the paint," Papa said. Johnny groaned. I was proud to think I was trusted with such a big job. I'd show everyone I was a perfect painter.

"Go with the grain," Papa said as he picked up a brush and demonstrated. "That way the paint will get in the cracks. Don't want the rain and snow to get in there. It'll rot the boards." Papa put Johnny on one side of the barn and me on the other. Good idea. Johnny and I could never work together without getting in an argument. I painted as fast as I could. After a couple of hours, my aching arm moved slower and slower. By breakfast time, I was exhausted, almost too tired to eat. Would I admit it? No sir! I somehow managed to down my potatoes, eggs, and bacon and get back to my job.

Around one o'clock, we stopped for dinner. I had switched to using my left hand. It didn't work to good, but my right arm throbbed. My fingers couldn't even hold the brush. Worst of all, I wasn't even halfway down the barn. It didn't seemed so big when we started. I was so used up, I fell asleep at the table.

I woke on my bed, confused. Where was I? How did I get here? Painting! I scrambled from my cot, ran outside, and began painfully brushing. I didn't get my side finished before it got dark. Papa said, "It's all right. Tomorrow's another day. You worked hard. I'm proud of you." I dropped into bed without supper or even putting on my nightdress.

Papa woke us at daybreak again. "Ohh!" I groaned. I hurt all over. Did I let a complaint slip past my lips? I could do this. I headed for the barn, donned my gunny sack, and went to work. The four bottom boards on my side of the barn were bright shiny red at the end of the second day. I pulled off the gunny sack and danced all the way to the house.

The next morning, as I rounded the corner of Johnny's side, he was just finishing up—the bottom four boards! "You painted my boards," I screamed. "Those are my boards! You're s'posed to do the high ones!"

Johnny grinned his crooked smile, "My arm got tired painting up there."

Pounding him with both fists, I screamed, "You painted my boards! My boards! Those were my boards!" He pushed me away like a horse swatting a fly while he giggled like a girl. Even I was amazed at my outburst. I'd been mad before but always let it boil inside like Mama's cooking pot. Guess the pot just boiled over.

I have to admit, my outburst felt good. The pot exploded. Anger instantly left me. I knew I'd have to apologize. Sad to say, that day launched a stream of temper eruptions, many embarrassing times, and hundreds of apologizes.

Papa came 'round the corner to see what the commotion was about. "John Westley," he said calmly, "looks like you've painted yourself into a problem. Now you've got the next four boards to paint all the way around. There's no way Susan can reach those. What was you thinkin', son?"

Johnny hollered, "I won't do it! You can't make me!" He threw the brush at Papa and tore up to the house yelling, "Mama!"

Not a word was said. Mama joined us in her old clothes. She brushed the upper four boards all the way around with powerful strokes. Johnny sat in his favorite dirt pile, playing with his homemade wooden cars. Mama and Papa didn't speak until the entire barn was a shiny, clean red.

Chapter 4

Where I Found Love

When Mama's month of bed rest after my birth was over, she set to tending the garden. Three-year-old Johnny went with her. Papa worked the fields. Mama's sister, Juna, often stopped by to help. Later, she shared stories of my early years with me.

I was left alone, sleeping in my box by the stove. I slept most of the time, but by the third month, my growing body would wake in ravenous hunger and whimper to an empty farmhouse. The whimper turned to a pathetic cry, followed by a full-blown, demanding scream. How long it went on depended on what Mama wanted to finish in the garden. Eventually she came to feed me, put me back in my box, and return to her work, irritated at being interrupted. By this time, the garden was ready to be harvested: vegetables picked and canned, pickles started, and fruit canned or made into jams and jellies. The winter food supply depended on how much Mama accomplished with garden produce in the months of August, September, and October.

By the beginning of September, I outgrew my sleeping box. Mama laid me on an old quilt by the edge of the garden under the shade of an apple tree where I could breathe fresh air and watched bugs, birds, and flowers.

Aunt Juna claimed Mama was happiest working in the garden, picking the abundant crops that thrived in the black fertile soil of the Camas Prairie. I seemed happiest lying in the shade, listening to the birds twitter, the *scritch, scritch* of the hoe taking out unwanted weeds, and, of all things, being entertained by my own Mama's passionate singing while she worked. She sang to no one in particular. Most of the time it was only my brother and me. "When Irish Eyes Are Smiling," "Too Ra Loo-Ra Loo Ra," and "In the Shade of the Old Apple Tree" were repeated over and over. The beautiful, sweet lilt of her Irish voice captivated me as I lay staring at the faded pattern on the old quilt. That was the beginning of my love for the outdoors. It held a side of my mother I never felt in the house.

Johnny helped pick a few things in the garden. He was three, and his interests were eating beans or peas and watching bugs. Mama gave him the job of picking the yellow, black, and white striped potato bugs off the vines and dropping them into the can she tied around his waist. Even that didn't hold his interest long. He'd sneak over to my blanket, take the bugs from the can, and drop them on me until I started crying or someone discovered what he was doing. He was jealous of the attention Papa gave me, so he clung to Mama. Mama tried to make up for lost Papa time by giving him whatever his heart desired. His heart certainly didn't desire farming.

It was Papa who held his baby girl close. He worked the fields up 'til dark each day, putting up hay for the animal's winter feed, harvesting grain, plowing some areas, and harrowing for spring planting. Even though he was tired from his dawn-to-dusk day walk behind the horses, he washed and picked me up from the baby box by the stove. He gently cuddled me close to his chest and sat in the old chair, humming and rocking.

He told me later this was the best part of his whole day. He carried on a conversation with me like I knew what he was talking about. "I worked with Kit and Bess on the South 40 today. Got about a third plowed. Probably two more days of plowin' 'til we can start harrowin'. Kit seemed a bit lame today, so I put some liniment on her left front leg tonight. Got a good price for the oats I took to town yesterday. Sorry I was late and didn't get to tell ya. It'll buy all we need of that new kind of barley seed for plantin' in the spring. Ya ought to see the taters your mama dug for supper. Real big and white through and through. Yes sir, that heavy rain we had in May certainly made a fine crop. We'll have plenty to eat this winter. You'll have your first taste of mashed taters come about Christmas. You'll love 'em."

He tracked my milestones in his diary. It was Papa who coaxed the first smile on my lips. It was Papa who was rewarded with my first laugh. He brought out babbling from my small tongue at the age of four months. As I watched his mouth moving above me in our daily conversations, "Papa" was, not surprisingly, my first real word. It was Papa who encouraged my first steps at the age of ten months.

From the time I could walk, Papa would take me into the fields. "Up you go," he called as he lifted me onto his lap in the seat of the harrow behind our two big brown horses, Kit and Bess. I'd squeal with delight as Papa called out, "Gee," and the horses threw their weight into the harnesses and began to move. "Whee," I'd call to the horses as I watched the tines of the harrow below Papa's feet dig into the ground, loosening it from its packed winter's rest. Ah, the rich smell of good black dirt still damp from the melted snows. It was like the earth's perfume calling out, "Come, work me, plow me, plant me, and I will give you a harvest of good things in return."

Papa's penetrating, secure love constantly assured me that he adored his black-eyed Susan. I, in turn, grew to love this man deeply.

Chapter 5

Baby, Berries, and Hard Times

In late June of 1918, I was picking strawberries. The patch was big, the berries were big, and so was my mama. She was going to have a baby. It was hard for her to get down to the ground, so I was the picker. I remember she had to lie down a lot. After all, she was forty-five years old. "That's old," I kept thinking. "Too old to have a baby."

Mama and Papa never told us about the baby. I guess things like that weren't talked about with kids. I found out one night when Grandmama and Grandpapa Denney came over to visit while we were still in our preparing season of the year. I'd already gone to bed and was about to drift off to sleep when suddenly my ears pricked up at something Grandpapa was yelling. "Yer gonna have another baby? Well, it's about time. Can't run a farm with only two kids. Ya need another good strong boy to make this work."

My eyes popped wide open. I held my breath and strained my ears to catch every word. I heard Mama go, "Shhhh! The children'll hear." Voices were lowered, and I could only make out bits and pieces of the rest of the conversation.

My thoughts were going wild. "A baby? Why would Mama have another baby when she never wanted me? Oh, no! If it's another boy, I'll be sandwiched and tortured from both sides. Things are going pretty good right now. A baby'll ruin everything."

Emotions swept through me like the train that roared through the edge of our land. It rumbled and shook the ground and threatened to run over me if I got in the way. Fear, jealousy, and worry threatened to stomp me over, and I could not get out of the way. I became invisible, pulling into a safe place. The news of a baby haunted me day and night.

These berries I was picking weren't just for us. I put them in big crocks that people dropped off, stored them in our cool dirt cellar under our house, and customers picked them up in the evening. I got five cents a day from the sale of our berries. Buyers would say to Papa, "I'd come ten miles just to get your berries, John. They're the sweetest, biggest, juiciest strawberries in all the county."

About halfway through strawberry picking season, on the day before my eighth birthday, I started not feeling good. "It's just the sun—too much sun," I told myself. "My head is aching 'cause I'm turned upside down all day with this picking."

The next day I had to pull myself out of bed. I hurt all over. I knew those big red berries were lying out there waiting for me. I couldn't even think of eating without getting nauseated, so I just kept picking all day. It was all I could do to drink a little water. That night I was shivering and sweating. When Papa woke me the next morning, he felt my forehead, looked at me with worried eyes, and shook his head, "Not today, black-eyed Susan. No pickin' today for you."

"No, Papa. I've got to. There's three crocks in the cellar." Papa shook his head again and woke up Johnny, sending him off to Grandma Kole's with a message to get Doc and have Papa's youngest sister come help with the picking.

I drifted back into a fitful dreaming sleep. I was picking . . . picking . . . picking. The smell of the berries was so powerful it smothered me. I tried holding my breath. I tried breathing through my mouth. It was like a huge strawberry blanket covered my bed. I woke gasping for air and found I was holding my nose. The nightmare didn't leave when I woke. Yes, all I could smell was strawberries! The door to the cellar was right under my window; today's picking was sending the aroma straight to my room. I began to retch and heave. Nothing came up.

The doctor didn't get there until after dinner. I was burning up. He took one look at me and told Papa, "Susan's got yellow jaundice. Look at her skin and eyes. See how yellow they are? She's running a mighty high temperature. We've got to get the temperature down." He gave me something in a spoon, sent Johnny to the well to get fresh water, wrapped me in cool, wet cloths, and I fell into darkness. The fight in me to go back to picking was gone. I slept. Doc stayed for three days. Every time I opened my eyes, he was sitting by my bed. It dawned on me, I was a very sick girl.

On the third day my fever broke. I stopped shivering and slept soundly. However, that didn't mean I was well. "It'll take months for her liver to heal. You're lucky she's alive. It's one of the worst jaundice cases I've seen," Doc told Papa and Mama. When he left, he gave directions for the medicine and promised to be back in four days.

He was right. I was so weak, I needed help getting from bed to bedpan. My head felt like bugs were eating my brain. My yellow skin was a sharp contrast to the white, homemade muslin sheets. I couldn't read. Getting up was out of the question. Eating was difficult. Talking seemed impossible; took too much effort. I slept. Doc came and went. I don't know how often. I don't remember much except my aching body and the horrible smell of strawberries.

Three weeks into this jaundice thing, I heard the door open downstairs and Doc's voice. I waited and waited, but he didn't come upstairs. Strange, I thought, and propped myself up far enough on one elbow to see out the one small window in my room. Yep, that was Doc's buggy and horse in the front yard.

My attention was suddenly pulled to voices in Papa and Mama's room directly below me. Mama screamed. What was wrong? Did Mama have the jaundice too? The doctor was giving Papa directions, Johnny was yelling and crying, and I was too weak to get more than a few steps from the bed. Fear invaded every part of me. What was happening?

After what seemed like hours of lying there listening to Mama scream and yell, I heard footsteps outside my room. Papa came in wearing a tired, worried look. "Mama's havin' a tough time with the baby. Just thought you ought to know what's goin' on," he muttered as he turned and went back down the narrow stairs.

"Oh no," my mind yelled. "What if something bad happens to Mama? It'll be my fault 'cause I don't want this baby." I couldn't do anything except lie there, cry, and ask God to help my mama.

Night came and then again morning. Still the cries of Mama shot through into my room. They seemed weaker now, more like the whining of a hurt dog. Suddenly, they became intense. Doc called for Papa, and a scream pierced the entire house, followed by another and another and another and then—a cry from a . . . a . . . yes . . . it was a baby! Mama was suddenly silent, and I heard Doc yelling for hot oil. Papa must have gotten it 'cause Johnny had run out of the house the day before and not come back.

My room was permeated with an overwhelming smell of cinnamon. It was ten times as bad as the strawberries. The odor sent my stomach into spasms. I was told later Mama bled profusely, and Doc used oil of cinnamon to stop the bleeding. Never have learned how.

I've never been able to eat anything with strawberries or cinnamon. I'm not allowed to donate blood. Yellow jaundice is now called hepatitis. What a traumatic summer it was for an eight-year-old; yellow jaundice, overpowering smells, and now, I was a big sister.

Chapter 6

My Harvest Job

The baby was a girl. They named her Agnes Edna. Guess there was enough money by then to give her two names. She had two traditional family names, just like John Westley. I was just plain Susan. Only one name—not even a family name. When I asked Papa why I only had one name, he explained, "Well, you see, when you were born we were too poor to give you two names. Your Grandpa Kole came over and the minute he saw you, he said, 'Well, hello there, little black-eyed Susan.'"

My aunts took turns coming to care for baby Edna, while Mama and I stayed in bed recuperating. I don't know what we'd have done without family around. Papa had to work the fields, and the care of the garden fell to Johnny. He whined and complained about that and the baby. "When I grow up, I'm never gonna be a farmer," he shouted at Papa. "I hate it, I hate you! And I'll never have no dumb baby!"

It turned out that 1918 was one of the most difficult years that Papa and Mama experienced on the farm. Hard times were expected back then. No quick fixes. Pioneer days had prepared them for anything. They never complained cause "that's just the way things were, no use complainin'." Papa would simply say, "The Lord'll see us through."

Area farmers, armed with scythes, arrived with wagons and teams in early September. For two days the army of workers fanned across the fields, cutting stalks of grain, bundling them with twine, and setting them up like guards. On the third day, they fired up the community-owned steam threshing machine, which huffed and puffed in the middle of the fields while men fed it bundles of grain from horse-drawn wagons. Grain spewed out a pipe on the other end where men caught it in gunny sacks, leaving just enough room to sew the top shut. When a waiting wagon was full of sacks, the driver and his team hauled them eleven miles to the flour mill in Reubens. Papa provided gunny sacks, twine, and needles for sewing.

From one hour after sunrise till one hour before sunset, the threshing crew toiled to get the crop in. It was long days for both humans and horses. Harvest never happened on Sunday. That was the day farmers rested and thanked the Lord.

By noon, the women of the host farmer had dinner ready to take to the field, where the workers ate in the shade under wagons. Seemed like farmers' wives had a competition going as to who could serve up the biggest and best. Harvest was hard work and brought on big appetites. It was nothing for the crew to devour three hams, two sacks of potatoes, twenty quarts of beans, six dozen homemade rolls, and ten apple pies in just one sitting. As soon as they finished eating and the dishes were done, the women started cooking for the next day.

Mama was up and working by then, but I was no help. I got downstairs by myself but didn't have strength. "I'll pull carrots and wash them," I told Mama. I got them pulled but couldn't carry them to the house. "Johnny! Come get the carrots," I yelled. Everyone had to work during harvest and guilt laid heavy on me. It had been my job the past two years to take drinking buckets from the well to the field several times a day. Not this year. Mostly I was just in the way.

On the second day of harvest, it dawned on me how I could help. "I'll take care of the baby," I told Mama.

"You sure I can trust you not to drop her?" she questioned. I nodded. "Here, sit in the rocker." With a pillow on my lap, I held baby Edna and sang every song I knew while Mama and two of her sisters cooked up a storm. Mama only stopped to feed her. I had found a place where I belonged—caretaker of my little sister. She loved me unconditionally.

Chapter 7

Back to School

Chesley school

At the beginning of October, Papa said, "Well, black-eyed Susan, come the first of November, Doc says you can go to school." School started the day after all farmers' fields were finished, usually around the middle of October. That allowed kids to help out with the threshing. I wouldn't be missing much schooling.

Johnny and I usually rode Old Bess four miles down the dirt road to the Chesley Schoolhouse. In winter, we'd snowshoe a shortcut across fields of snow higher than the fence posts.

Johnny soaked his hair every morning so he could comb it straight back. One day in January of 1917, Mama told him, "Johnny, you can't do that when it's fifteen degrees below zero." He paid her no mind. The ice-crusted snow was slick under our snowshoes. Bitter cold cut my breath short, numbed my cheeks and nose, and by the time we got to school, I couldn't feel my toes.

While we were hanging our coats, Johnny's friend Clyde greeted him, "Hey, Johnny, how come the white hair? You turn old overnight?" He jokingly slapped my brother's frozen hair. With a strange crunching sound, it broke, falling to the floor like shards of glass. We all laughed— except Johnny. His thawed hair stuck out in all directions. Mama knitted a stocking cap, which he wore until June, even in the house.

One year, Papa made short, wooden skis and we traveled the two miles of pure white world with great speed. This year was different. I wasn't strong enough for snowshoes or skis. Papa hitched up the sleigh, and ol' Bess pulled us with warm rocks under our feet and lap robes covering our legs. What luxury!

It was my third class year. I knew how to read, write, add, subtract, multiply, and was working on division. I loved spelling. Many schoolmates were my cousins, but I had a special friend named Avis. We were two peas in a pod.

"It's time," I whispered. "Let's go," would be the response. We climbed into the rafters of the coatroom and made ourselves comfortable.

"We need to study for the geography test for tomorrow," Avis stated.

"You first," I began. "What's the name of the tallest mountain in the world? Where is the biggest desert found? What continent is surrounded by water?" We quizzed each other until we were sure we both knew the answers.

The teacher was busy with other kids in our one-room school. Each day we drilled each other on spelling words, math facts, history, or English. No, we didn't always stick to the subject. Sometimes, girl giggles took over, and we'd almost fall off our rafters.

The one outside door of Chesley school opened into the coatroom, which also held stacks of wood the older boys cut before going home each day. A small arch led into class. In winter, a thick quilt hung across it to keep out the cold. Teacher's desk sat at the front of the room, and students' desks were grouped according to age in the corners of the room. Our teacher moved from group to group, giving lessons, but sat at her desk to teach us individually. We had anywhere from twenty-five to thirty kids depending on who had moved to the Reubens school for ninth grade. My teacher was married to my uncle Willie. Her name was Aunt Bertha, but I had to call her Mrs. Kole.

In the center of the room sat a black, potbellied stove. A big pot of "something" was always simmering our lunch. Avis and I played a game of "guess by the smell what's for lunch" as we took off our coats. "It's stew," I would announce. "No, it's not," she'd counter, "it's ham and beans." Whatever it was, it was always delicious, hot, and filling. Food was provided by students' families, but the teacher decided what to make with it. She got there early to start the fire and put the pot on. We took turns doing the dishes and cleaning up.

I loved learning. I soaked up whatever I heard or read. That was good. I didn't realize my school days would be limited to eight years. I wasn't allowed to go to secondary school in Reubens because I didn't have proper shoes. No shoes and only one name? Johnny and Edna attended high school. Both dropped out before graduating. It hardly seemed fair, but then hadn't I learned from the very beginning that life isn't fair?

Knowing how hungry I was to learn, Aunt Bertha gave me a book each year for my birthday. She even lent me books from her collection. I memorized every page. On the year I turned thirteen, she gave me a Bible. I was excited. "This is great," I exclaimed. "Now I can read for myself what Grandma and Grandpa Kole used to learn to speak English." They both were raised in a community in Holland, Michigan, where only Dutch had been spoken and written. When they married, they decided they must learn the American language of English. Grandma held a Dutch Bible and Grandpa an English Bible. Verse by verse, they learned to read and speak the words in English. I loved talking with them about things in the Bible—always in English. Once they learned English, they never spoke Dutch again. "When in America, we must always speak the American language," Grandpa would say when I would ask him a word in Dutch.

Aunt Bertha died from cancer in August after I turned sixteen. My heart broke. She believed in me and had been my champion, giving me through books a picture of life beyond the farm. The most precious book she'd bequeathed to me was my Bible. It held hope for the future. All would turn out right because "through Christ I can do all things." Yes, I believed that.

Chapter 8

The Telephone

A marvelous invention arrived called the telephone. Lines were strung through the farmlands of the Camas Prairie when I was nine.

Papa said, "Of course, we want a telephone. It'll be handy to talk to the folks. Save lots of time." Papa was always keen on new inventions. Mama not. She feared the new. Maybe because she had been uprooted by her father at the age of eight to come West in a wagon train, or maybe because she was eight years older than Papa.

Papa and Johnny set eight, twelve-foot poles along the quarter mile from the road to our house. Workmen attached the line and hooked up the phone on the kitchen wall. The brown wooden box had an attached megaphone to speak into and a receiver hooked to a cord for listening. How exciting to hear my grandparents' voices on the other end of that line. Johnny and I weren't allowed to call, but we could talk if an adult was visiting with someone. It crackled and sputtered, sometimes cutting the conversation short. It was a miracle to be connected by a wire to someone three miles away. Yes, a real miracle.

One mid-September day, Mama, Papa, and Johnny hitched up the wagon and headed for the field to gather the last crop of hay. It was a short growing season at our elevation, and every bit of food for both animals and people was cherished. Dark clouds began gathering out west. They were moving with the speed of—oh no, lightning! They didn't make it to the barn before the storm attacked. Lightning struck the fast-moving wagon, hitting the metal brads that held together the horses' harnesses, sending sparks flying into the air. It made hair stand out in every direction and bounced off the metal axles of the wagon. "Why it didn't kill us or those horses, I'll never know," Papa later recalled. "Sparks were shooting everywhere."

Meanwhile, I'd seen the storm coming and hurried little fourteen-month-old Edna into the house, shutting up windows as a fierce wind began to blow. As I came downstairs to the kitchen, Edna was sitting on the floor, playing with her sock teddy bear. We were safe from the storm. I worried about the rest. Were they still out in the field? Had they seen the storm in time to get in?

Cr-a-a-c-k! Without warning, a blaze of fire shot from the telephone streaking to the wood cook stove on the other side of the kitchen—right over Edna's head. *Ka-boom!* The house shook like a dancing skeleton. "Help!" I screamed, grabbing Edna and running out the door. "No place is safe! No place is safe!" I yelled. "The barn, the barn . . ." The barn had a lightning rod on top. It was supposed to keep the barn from getting struck. If we could just get to the barn. With Edna tight in my arms, I hurled myself across the grass and barnyard to the door that was only open wide enough to squeeze through. I threw myself and shrieking Edna onto the fresh hay. A big familiar hand gently shook my shoulder, "Are you two all right?"

Chapter 9

Mable

It became my job to take Edna off Mama's hands when I got home from school. I taught her new words, played with her, helped her learn to walk, sang to her, and told her stories; whenever I could get a book, I read to her. It wasn't a chore to take care of my little sister. I loved her so much. She loved me back. I wanted at least six kids when I grew up.

I never received a Christmas gift, except the usual orange, candy, and nuts sent by Uncle Martin who lived in California. Some years there might be a pair of homemade slippers or much-needed work boots for going to the chicken pen or sometimes a new pair of mittens or scarf.

When I was nine years of age, my stocking on Christmas morning held the most beautiful china doll I'd ever seen. She had black hair like mine, brown eyes, and a beautiful, white porcelain face with rosy, pink cheeks. I named her Mable. I hugged her tight and cried, "Oh, thank you, thank you, thank you!"

"You take good care of Edna," Papa said. "We thought you were old enough to take care of a doll. You have to be very careful with her. She'll break easy."

"I will, I will," I promised. Mable stayed in my room most of the time, keeping me company as I fell asleep and watching me all through the night. She was my greatest treasure.

Two years passed. In the summer, Mama worked in the field with the crew or cooked the noon meal. Edna, now three, was a busy little girl. I took care of her from the time she got up until bedtime. I hoped it was a big help to Mama, but she never made any comment or even said "thank you."

Johnny hated every minute he had to work in the fields. He'd rather be whittling, writing stories, or learning to play his banjo, a twelfth birthday gift. So when there was a crew working our farm, he'd sneak off and work his way back to the house.

"What are you doing here?" I demanded on one of his escape days. "You're in the field today."

"You're not going to tell me what to do."

"I'll tell Papa you snuck away."

"You just keep your mouth shut or I'll. . ."

"You'll what?"

"You'll be sorry you were ever born."

"It isn't right you don't do your share of the work. Papa works hard so you get stuff like your old banjo. You get everything you want, but you won't work for it!" By this time I was losing my temper.

"It's none of your business what I do or what I get!"

He ran up to my room, grabbed Mable and yelled as he ran out the door, "I'm taking her. You'll never get her back."

I tore after him screaming, "No, no, not Mable. Please, not Mable. Please give her back."

He climbed to the top of the chicken coop with his hostage, ignoring my pleas and shouted, "Don't ever boss me around again!" He threw her to the ground, shattering her head, hands and feet into many pieces. His devious act broke through to my very soul. I lay on the ground moaning over the loss of my most prized possession.

"Now, I bet you're so mad that you'd just like to go stuff yourself with bananas," he yelled as he stomped into the house.

I never told and no one ever asked what happened to Mable.

Chapter 10

Automobiles and Airplanes

Living in the country had advantages. I loved the outdoors, working in the dirt, watching things grow, picking wild flowers, swimming in the pond, ice skating, and skiing in the winter. The quiet. Ah, the quiet. Time to think, time to imagine, time to plan.

The summer I turned twelve, my quiet time in the garden thinning radishes was suddenly interrupted by a strange sound; nothing like anything I'd ever heard. I stood, shaded my eyes, and stared all around. It seemed to be coming from the direction of the road.

"What's that sound, Johnny?"

"Gosh if I know," he answered, dropping the horse's feed bucket. We ran toward the road full speed as the noise got louder and louder. It was coming from a huge dust ball rolling down the road.

"It's an automobile!" yelled Johnny. "I heard the Rosenkranzes got one of those horseless things." He started running again.

Mama came out of the house screaming, "Johnny, Susan, get in this house! Get in this house! Now!"

Johnny stopped, looked at me, and shook his head. "Mama's scared of it. She heard one got away and ran into a house." We both looked back the quarter mile down our little road, torn between obeying our Mama and seeing this automobile for ourselves. It sputtered and popped its way past the end of our road; we turned and walked back to our Mama who was still standing on the porch screaming.

"When I say get in the house, you get in the house. You hear? You'll get run over by that new fang-dangled contraption. Don't ever go near one. You hear?"

"Yes, Mama," we replied, knowing we'd jump at the chance to see one.

That next chance came at the Fourth of July picnic at Winchester Lake. There it sat. An amazing, open air machine painted black with real leather seats. Four people could fit inside. Mr. Rosenkranz was giving rides. What a thrill! How could Mama say no when everybody, large and small, was taking him up on it. We putted around the lake trail no faster than we could walk, but we didn't have to do a thing. I was fascinated by the levers and buttons, but most of all how the wheel inside made the wheels outside go the direction he wanted.

Johnny was more than fascinated; he was obsessed. He hounded Papa from that day on until finally, when he turned sixteen, Papa bought a Model T. It held only two passengers and had a box on the back so things could be hauled in it. That made it farm practical as well as an extravagance. People could always ride in the back if need be.

The next year, another unfamiliar sound shattered our calm countryside. Those Rosenkranzes! Don't know where he got money for all these new gadgets, but there he was flying an airplane right over our house. Mama came tearing out of the house screaming and yelling, but we couldn't hear. We stood looking up with our mouths open. Unbelievable. A machine that could fly through the air and hold people, too. We'd heard about such a thing on the radio. Once I remember looking at pictures in a newspaper someone brought from Lewiston. Those pictures now became reality.

Mama was frantic. Where could she hide her family from such danger? Even if she corralled us all in the house or barn, the plane could hit the buildings. How could she keep us safe? I saw sheer terror on her face. I ran from the tree where I'd been picking apples and threw my arms around her as she collapsed on the ground sobbing. My mama was crying. I loved my mama. She wanted to keep me safe. That must mean she loved me too. But I received no return hug.

Chapter 11

If You Knew Susie Like I Know Susie

There were two seasons on the farm—the working season from April through October and the preparing season November through March. Preparing season was when kids went to school, grain sacks were mended, clothes were sewn and patched, plows and harrows were cleaned and sharpened, and repairs were done to buildings. Most importantly, we took out time to have some fun.

Literaries—now those were some good times! There isn't any such thing today. It was drama, performance, sing-a-longs, and comedians all rolled into one. The whole farm community would gather at the Chesley Schoolhouse on the first Saturday of the month, bringing a covered dish and something to perform after the feast. I'll never forget one literary when my cousin Boyd was about eight years old; he got up to do a speaking piece. He cleared his throat, "Ahump," and loudly recited. "Cream of Wheat is really neat. It makes you big and fat. If I eat my Cream of Wheat, will I be as big as that?" and he pointed right at Mrs. Zhalber, who was a very large lady. He finished, bowed, and there was utter silence. No one knew what to do. Suddenly there was this gurgling sound coming from Mrs. Zhalber in the front row. When we realized she was laughing, we all joined her and it brought down the house. After that, Boyd's mom always checked his material beforehand.

Sometimes, the food would be in the form of a box social. All the women and older girls would bring a box filled with their best cooking. They'd go to great lengths to make the box attractive to the men who would be bidding. Each cook was extremely secretive in getting her box to the schoolhouse so bidders had no idea who made it. Not even husbands knew what their wife's box looked like. At the last "sold" announcement, each bidder claimed his box and the men formed a big circle around the room and the women faced them. The women walked around the inside circle clapping hands to music. The music stopped and the women scrambled around the room to claim their box and their eating partner. Kids always ate with their mother and the person who bought her box. All money from the box social went to the schoolhouse to help buy books and supplies and pay the teacher's salary.

Schoolhouse dances were held on the other Saturdays. This entertainment was common in small rural communities. In fact, Mama and Papa met at the dance in Tekoa, Washington, when she was fifteen and he was seven. Papa took a liking to that beautiful, auburn-haired young woman. It was probably infatuation. After all, Minnie was eight years older. She was, however, willing to become a little girl long enough to dance with a handsome seven-year-old boy. Papa claimed it was true love.

Any local musician was welcomed to play at these schoolhouse jam sessions. They got together on Friday nights to practice and learn new tunes they heard on the radio. That invention changed not only the tunes but the style of music and the new steps. It seemed there was always someone who had been in Lewiston and picked up the latest.

Music seemed to follow my family's life. During my teen years, my brother, Johnny, began courting a girl named Frankie. They seemed a great fit. The folks liked her. Six months into their courting, a new song hit the radio. The first line went: "Frankie and Johnny were sweethearts . . ." Of course, they heard that song from everyone, everywhere they went. At first it was fun, eventually it became irritating, and finally wore them out along with their interest in each other. But that's another story.

Not long after that, another song was heard on our scratchy airwaves, "If you knew Susie, like I know Susie, oh, oh, oh what a gal . . ." It followed me around like a faithful dog. The local musicians, always quick to pick up a new catchy tune, were soon playing it, and we were two-stepping it at the local dances.

The Nolan family, with eight kids, lived on a farm not far from the schoolhouse. One was named Walt. He made it his mission to always ask me to dance during the "Susie" song then sang it the whole time. I got so tired of that song—and Walt. I even stayed home one night pretending to be sick so I wouldn't have to dance with him. I would never have thought of saying no when he asked me to dance. I'd been taught by Mama to be a good girl and always be polite.

Years later, after my husband died, Walt came from his home in Walla Walla to see me a couple of times. On his third visit, he said, "Susie, since your husband has died and my wife has died, how about marrying me?" When I looked at him, that song flew back into my mind, "If you knew Susie like I know Susie . . ." The old irritation flew back too. I said, "No, I've been there and done that." He looked me straight in the eye and said, "Okay, then I'll ask Vada. I know she'll say yes."

Chapter 12

Cousin Clothes

Uncle Martin had moved to California leaving farm life because of allergies, but the other Kole and Denney brothers and sisters still farmed the Reubens area. When both sides of my family got together, there were around sixty people, lots of cousins to play with. We jammed into one of the grandparents' houses, ate until we were stuffed, and all talked at once. It was a noisy, happy time. Nothing was more important than the big family. I felt like I belonged there.

Toward evening we snacked on leftovers and instruments appeared. I'm not sure if my grandparents brought them when they came West or if they eked out enough extra on the farm to buy the precious fiddles, viola, piano, guitars, banjos and base fiddle. Come to think of it, both grandfathers played at schoolhouse dances when they lived in Tekoa; they must have brought their fiddles with them.

The musicians gathered around the dining room tuning up, while we cleared the sitting room of all furniture. The wild, merry music began. Everyone danced, from the youngest to the oldest; square dances, round dances, fox trots, two-steps, and later on, even the Charleston. When dancers had to catch their breath, the musicians would switch to songs we could sing: "You are My Sunshine," "Down in the Valley," "My Wild Irish Rose," "America," "Red Wing," "I've Been Working on the Railroad," and "Oh Susanna." I'm sure we were heard ten miles down the road at the next farmhouse.

Mama's side of the family had four girl cousins within a year of each other: Katherine, Beth, Hazel, and me. Beth's Papa died in the war and her grieving Mama hung herself. At six years old, Beth came to live with Grandmama and Grandpapa. When we weren't dancing, we hid away in one of the many bedrooms in their house and giggled about things that were funny only to us. In our teens, of course, it was girl talk about boys.

Grandmama Denney often made cousin dresses from the same pattern so we looked like quadruplets. That made us feel even more connected. Strangers usually thought we were sisters and constantly got our names mixed up. Making dresses was a long process of stitching by hand. In 1918, however, a modern invention made life easier when Grandmama got a brand-new treadle sewing machine from the Montgomery Ward's catalogue. She whizzed up dresses in no time.

Our school dresses were made from flour sacks. You see, flour came in cloth bags in those days; not just any cloth bag, but ones with beautiful printed patterns. Even though we raised wheat, we still had to buy flour after it was ground. We made our own bread and used around three hundred pounds a year. It was exciting to go to town with Papa on a flour-buying trip twice a year to pick out the kind of sack I wanted for a dress. It took two fifty-pound sacks to make a dress. When I was mostly grown, the flapper style had taken over and dresses were very short, so it still only took two fifty-pound sacks. I had two school dresses: one to be washed, starched, and ironed while I was wearing the other. I always changed into my housedress and apron when I got home to keep my dress clean enough to wear to school all week.

House dresses were ankle length and covered by a wide bibbed apron. The aprons, dresses, skirts, and blouses worn at home were what we called reworked clothes. Mama would cut up old outgrown dresses and sew the pieces together, creating something modest and suitable for working. Sometimes she even had enough left over to make a dress for little Edna.

Our families saved all year to get store-bought cloth to make matching dresses for us four cousins to wear on the Fourth of July. It was sometimes hard to estimate size with the sewing being done in winter. I remember one year, I took a growing spurt. My dress was so tight come July, I could hardly breathe, let alone eat picnic dinner. It quickly became part of a house dress.

The celebration on Independence Day was second only to Christmas. Each family prepared a basket of their favorite food, dressed in their finest to honor the birth of our country, and made their way as fast as the old horses could pull the buggies over to Winchester Lake.

One year at age eleven, we cousins rode over with Grandmama and Grandpapa. We were excited and wanted to hurry. Every once in a while, we'd drop a hint to Grandpapa, "Is this all the faster old Pat can go? Does Pat have a bad leg? I don't think you gave old Pat his oats this morning." Finally, Grandpapa cleared his throat and announced, "Girls, 'tis no use of hurrying 'cause nothing's going to happen 'till we get there." We never pushed him again.

Winchester, a small logging town, was the hub of the community. People from all over the Camas Prairie would fill the split log tables and benches set up around the lake. It was a day to forget about work, stuff ourselves with shared food, visit with old friends, and make new ones. It began when we got there all right, and didn't stop until way after dark when fireworks was set off over the lake. We didn't care how long it took to get back home because we were sleeping. It's a good thing old Pat knew the way home because I suspect even the driver nodded off.

At seventeen, we cousins bought winter coats alike. It was a good harvest and all of us sewed sacks for threshing crews to make some money of our own. "Look," suggested Katherine, "we're not gonna grow anymore so we can wear these coats for 20 years." That was my first piece of store-bought clothing! I can still see us in those ankle-length black coats with big fur collars and our round, tight-fitting bucket hats. We thought we were "the cat's meow." That was the last time we dressed alike.

Chapter 13

Sweet Sixteen

When I turned sixteen, the Kole and Denney families came to our house for dinner—unusual for summer birthdays. It was warm enough to set up sawhorses and planks outside. Everyone piled their food offering on it. Children always got to go first at family meals. Uncle Willie, who had become a minister, said our blessing. "And bless our little black-eyed

Susan," he ended. That made me feel very special. No one had ever prayed for me in public before.

"Let's go up to your room," Catherine said after we were so full we couldn't move. "I want to talk." So we four cousins headed up the stairs.

Our house was anything but soundproof with only sawdust and newspaper for insulation in the walls, but not in the floor. Below we could hear laughing, talking, and scraping of furniture.

"Hmm. Must be getting ready to dance," I commented.

"'Spec so," replied Beth. The girls rolled their eyes at each other. Seemed strange.

They kept talking about nothing important. Pretty soon, Papa called me, "Susan you're needed down here."

"Sorry, I'd better go," I apologized. "Do you get to stay overnight?" They all nodded and I headed down the narrow stairway. When I reached the kitchen and rounded the corner into the dining room, I was surprised by the absence of instruments. I could have sworn I heard furniture being moved.

"Over here," I heard my little sis call. I walked into an emptied sitting room made ready for a dance. Strange. Everyone just stood there watching me. Even stranger. I felt uncomfortable being the center of attention. I heard Papa say, "Ready, set, go!" Everyone shouted, "Surprise!" The right side of the room parted and there was a real Silvertone phonograph from the Montgomery Ward's catalogue, sitting on a homemade brown cabinet with the door open, revealing ten black 78 records! My phonograph that I had longed for, torn the page out of the catalogue, and pinned by my bed, but knowing we could never afford it—there it was! I couldn't believe it. Someone pushed the "on" lever and set the needle to the already wound player. Papa said, "May I have the first dance?" The orchestra burst forth with the Blue Danube, and my papa and I, with tears in our eyes, waltzed around the room while everyone swayed.

Having received my eighth grade diploma at the age of 14, I was in training for being a housewife. I wasn't allowed to go on to high school because I didn't need that much education. Besides, remember, I didn't have proper shoes to go to Reubens school. I was the first of the four cousins to turn sixteen. Sixteen, the magical age when a young lady was considered marriageable.

The families had pooled their money to buy my precious record player. Papa had lovingly made the cabinet on which it sat. I felt so loved. Family get-togethers were times I felt in the right place. My grandparents, aunts, uncles, and especially my papa and little sister loved me. My cousins and I were close friends.

However, I was sharply aware of the absence of my mother. I heard her clanging things in the kitchen; couldn't be bothered with the silliness of celebrating sixteen. When the laughter faded along with the music, I slipped back into my own private world, trying to find a way to make Mama love me too.

Chapter 14

The Preacher's Coming

The schoolhouse was home to many events in our farm community. The most exciting time was late fall after harvest when the itinerant preacher came riding on his horse and held gospel meetings. At sixteen, I'd heard many preachers who rode through, staying for a few days. This year was different. There were two men. They came in a horse-drawn buggy. Albert F. Gray was the preacher. Mr. Hollingsworth led the singing. Two men came to our small community to teach us about God and sing with us? How exciting!

Every morning around nine o'clock, after the milking and chores were done, we packed a basket lunch, piled in the wagon, and headed for the schoolhouse. Families took turns getting there first to build the fire. Since everyone farmed, nine o'clock to three o'clock was the perfect timing.

Promptly at nine-thirty, Mr. Hollingsworth began singing. Oh, how he could sing! There were no instruments except our voices shaking the rafters. They brought small songbooks with them. Most hymns were familiar, but some were new. One new song grabbed my attention, "I Am a Child of God." My mind was spinning. What does that mean? "I have washed my robes in the cleansing fountain. I am a child of God." If I listen closely to preacher Gray, maybe he will tell me.

After an hour of hardy singing, Mr. Hollingsworth gathered the songbooks and preacher Gray stood up, Bible in his hand and a smile on his face. "Morning folks," he started. "We've come to share the gospel with you. It's the story of God coming down so we can go up to Him." He began reading in the book of Genesis. *What?* I thought. *Grandma Kole said the gospels were Matthew, Mark, Luke, and John.*

Reverend Gray read, "In the beginning God created the heaven and the earth."

Yes, I knew that. I'd read about that in my own Bible Aunt Bertha had given me.

"You see, man was created in God's image. He put man, Adam, into a perfect garden." I had read this story and heard it from Grandma and Grandpa Kole. *Why was he starting at the beginning? I wanted the important part of the story—the part about being God's child.* As preacher Gray spun the story of creation, my mind begin to wander. *Was it too hot in here or is that just me? I should have eaten more breakfast; my stomach's growling.*

"There was this snake also in the garden," he was saying. I shuddered. *I do not like snakes. I've had to kill timber rattlers when we were down in the canyons. I can't see how Eve even wanted to talk to it. It must have had powerful charm.*

He continued, "It was the devil disguised with a deceitful wise-sounding tongue." *Well, you wouldn't have caught me listening to him—snake, no; devil, mercy no! I would have run.*

"Eve was persuaded to do the wrong thing," the preacher was saying. "Have you noticed how it's easier to do the wrong thing than it is to do the right thing? That's because on that day, in the beginning of earth's days, the devil became the ruler of people's hearts. Ever since, man has been cursed and bent to do evil. Our hearts are evil."

Not mine, I thought, *I've tried all my life to do the right thing, to be the good girl, to make people proud of me. My heart isn't evil.* As we traveled home in the buggy, I was consumed with the thought, *"Could there be evil in my heart?"*

Chapter 15

The Second Day of Meetings

Sleeping was difficult that night. I lay there wondering about an evil heart. Preacher Gray had left me in the middle of the air. It was like he condemned me and then said, that's all there is to it. I had a lot of questions. I couldn't ask God. I was told by Uncle Willie, "You never question God. He's the Almighty and what He said is true." Besides, how would God answer me?

I could ask the preacher. Wasn't that his job, to tell me if I was right or wrong? I wanted to know when evil came into my heart. How come I didn't know it was there? I tried hard to do the right thing. What could I do about the evil? Was the devil still around? I don't know what he looks like, but I don't think he's still a snake. I've seen lots of snakes on our farm. None of them ever talked to me.

Morning came early, but not early enough for me. I hopped out of bed, dressed, gobbled down my breakfast, and finished my chores long before time to leave. "You're unusually quiet this morning, Susan," Papa observed. "Are you all right?"

"Yes, Papa, I just want to get to the preaching service on time."

"Hmm. Is there a special reason? Got an eye on one of those young fellows that came to the meetin' yesterday?" he asked.

"Oh, Papa. You know that's not true." I blushed. Ever since June, everyone kept dropping hints about me having a guy. There were no guys around our area I would want to get serious about. Just because I was sixteen didn't mean I'd go out and fall in love.

I helped Papa hitch up Old Kit. As we trotted along the frozen dirt road, I started questioning my questions. What if the preacher thinks my questions are simple-minded? What if he says I'm too young to understand? What if he laughs at my questions and says, "What a curious question, young lady?" I had a man teacher who did that. One year, Aunt Bertha was sick; he finished our school year for her. He didn't like questions. He would comment about me, but never answered my questions. He often laughed at me like I was there to amuse him. I quit asking questions. No, I decided. I won't ask the preacher my questions. I'll just listen.

There were two buggies at the schoolhouse when we arrived. One was the Nolans' who were the fire-starters for the day, and the other belonged to the family of my best friend, Avis. She ran out the door and gave me a hug. It was good to see her. Since I wasn't allowed to go on to the ninth grade in Reubens, I hadn't seen Avis much the last year and half. We hurried inside the warming schoolhouse and huddled in a corner of the room to catch up on news.

"Susan," her eyes sparkled, "I've met the nicest guy. He's going to graduate from high school this year. He's funny and smart, a slick dresser, and he already has a job after school."

"Really?" I questioned. How could my friend be so head-over-heels with a guy she'd only known a year and a half? She hardly knew him. He was so much older than her.

"And here's the best part, my parents think he's a dear. They invite him to dinner at least one night a week." Avis's family moved into town after she left Chesley school so she'd have a better social life.

Of course that didn't happen in my case. I was expected to be a wife and mother, so education and social life came second to my home training. However, it didn't slow down my brother's social life. He talked Papa and Mama into getting a Model A Ford. He drove it to school until he dropped out in eleventh grade. After that, every weekend he traveled to Reubens or Gifford or Winchester to pursue his other interest—girls.

"He's tall. I only come up to his shoulder," Avis continued. Now that wouldn't be very tall since Avis was only five feet two inches. Talk about songs following you; "Five foot two, eyes of blue, could she, could she, could she coo! Has anybody seen my gal?" was her theme song. "He's got brown hair, blue eyes and he wants six kids."

"Avis!" I said a bit too loud. Everyone turned and looked at us. "Sorry," I apologized, continuing in a whisper, "you've talked about how many kids you want?"

"Of course we have, I think he's going to ask me to marry him." I was stunned.

A crowd had gathered, and Mr. Hollingsworth was passing out songbooks. Avis and I quickly took our places on an empty bench. The singing began. My mind reeled from Avis's news. It was unexpected. I couldn't picture my best friend getting married, even though she was a year older than me. My thoughts raced to the future. *This is only the beginning,* I thought. *Avis, my cousins, me. The future? What's going to happen to all of us? Will we still live here? Can we still be friends if we get married? Will we all get married? Who will be my husband? Where will I live? How many children will I have?*

Lost in my musing, I suddenly became aware I wasn't singing. I glanced around, turned to the right page, and began to sing. It wasn't until the last song that my mind came completely back to the present. "I have washed my robes in the cleansing fountain, I am a child of God."

Chapter 16

Freedom!

"Yesterday," began preacher Gray, "we talked about how sin came. How we are the children of sin because of Eve and Adam disobeying God in the Garden of Eden. It was their choice. They chose to do the wrong thing. After they were driven out of the beautiful garden, they had children. Their first two were boys. The oldest boy demonstrated an evil heart. Cain became jealous and angry at his younger brother, Abel. He let it control him and he killed Abel and left him in the field. Where did the sin in his heart come from? From his parents' disobedience . . ."

Preacher Gray continued his review, and my mind was saying, *Yes, I get jealous too. I've never told anyone. Mama wouldn't think I was a good girl if she knew how jealous I was of all the money they spend on Johnny. Whatever Johnny wants, Johnny gets: a bicycle, a banjo, store-bought ice skates instead of Papa's homemade ones, the Model A Ford, store-bought clothes, an accordion, a fancy cane. I could go on and on. Johnny runs away on some special errand every time he's asked to do any work. Besides all that, he went to high school in Reubens while I had to stay home and learn to be a housewife. You bet I'm jealous. As long as I hadn't killed him, it surely wasn't a sin—although at times I wished I could.*

There are lots of ways people do the wrong thing: killing, stealing, lying, cheating. The list is in the Ten Commandments I memorized in school. I'd followed them. I didn't break them. I wanted to be a good girl, and God said to keep them. I didn't worship an idol; I didn't even own one. Our family worshiped on Sunday; not always in church because we didn't have one. I never, ever took God's name in vain. Nice girls don't swear. I always did what Mama and Papa told me to do. The last one? Well, I may have coveted just a little, but not enough that I would steal.

"Proverbs chapter twenty-three and verse seven," announced preacher Gray. It brought me out of my recollection and back to the schoolhouse. "A simple short thought," he said. "Let's read it together."

"For as he thinks in his heart, so is he," everyone intoned.

What? No, no, no. That can't be true! My mind was denying. *No one knows. I've never told anyone. It's my secret!*

Preacher Gray continued, "You see, God knows our heart. He knows our thoughts. He understands we're sinners. He loves us anyway and wants you and me to be His child—a child of God. But we can't be His child with sin in our hearts. The devil deceives us. Whispers 'You're not so bad. You've never done anything that's hurt someone. You try to be good and do all the right things.'" It was like the preacher was reading my thoughts. Had I been talking out loud? I glanced quickly around, but no one was looking at me.

"All you have to do is believe in Jesus. Admit you're a sinner, ask Him to forgive your sins and cleanse you from all unrighteousness."

Mr. Hollingsworth began to sing, "Will you come to Jesus? He is calling . . ."

Verse after verse, they sang for a half hour. People went forward and knelt at the old school bench in front. People cried and called out to God. People asked forgiveness and gave their hearts to Jesus. There was power in the room, like God had a string attached pulling us toward Him. I couldn't summon the courage to go forward. I'd always been a private person. Maybe it's pride, maybe it's shyness. I closed my eyes, shut my ears to the music and crying, and talked to God while sitting on my own hard bench. *God, I've tried to be good. I've followed all your laws. I still sin. My thoughts are mean and wicked, and I can't control them. Forgive me. Make me your child.* With that simple prayer, I felt a weight lift, a peace enter, and a new joy I never felt before. I knew Jesus' spirit lived in me. I was free!

Chapter 17

The Storm

The change may not have been too evident, but I was free and happy for the first time. My attitude toward Johnny and Mama changed. I loved them with my entire being. Maybe this was what would build a bridge between Mama and me? Is this the miracle I've been waiting for? She didn't change. She was still curt and abrupt. There was no conversation, just orders and I was expected to do as I was told without compliments or praise. Johnny was still selfish, mean, and said hurtful things. The change was the song inside of me, "I am a child of God!" He loved me and that's all that mattered.

The meetings lasted another four days. I soaked up all I could about what this change meant and what it looked like in real life. I floated on a cloud. I was going to be with God forever. His promise was rooted in my heart!

Edna was in school, and Johnny went off looking for jobs or courting some girl. That left me home with Mama and Papa to do winter chores and keep the house clean. It gave me time to ask questions. Mama didn't like questions, but Papa was always up to telling stories that held the answers. I also trudged across the snow to Grandma and Grandpa Kole's, helping them around the house and bombarding them with questions.

Papa's younger brother, Jim, married a lady named Grace Chase. She came from Clearwater, a small town about a day's buggy ride from us. They, along with their son, Boyd and daughter, Belledene, lived on

Grandma and Grandpa Kole's original homestead about two miles from us. I often visited them. Grace had a strong faith like Grandma and Grandpa Kole. We talked about my hard questions. Aunt Grace told me, "Cast your cares on Him because He cares for you." Fear still visited the corners of my mind and tried to bring back failure and rejection.

The next two years were personally uneventful, except for one tragic day. Mama sent me to Uncle Jim and Aunt Grace's with a cake she'd baked for their anniversary. I stayed a while and played with my little cousins. We were sitting by the front window eating popcorn when suddenly Belledene cried, "Look! A funny cloud."

Indeed, it was a funny-looking cloud. It was shaped like a cone they put ice cream in at the Fourth of July picnic, except this was black and moving around. "I've never seen one like that before," I commented. "Let's go find your mama." Just then, Aunt Grace came blowing in the door; her hair stood straight up from the wind.

"Come! We've got to go to the root cellar!" she called. The urgency in her voice didn't leave any room for questions. We followed her quickly. I don't remember how long we stayed there.

She called it a tornado. "They sometimes dip down and touch the ground," she explained. "When it does, it's mighty destructive."

"Are we safe in here?" I was very nervous. Other than thunder and lightning, I'd never seen weather that I had to be afraid of.

"We're safe, but we need to pray for the people in the fields and the ones below the cloud." She prayed. Belledene, Boyd, and I huddled together, shaking in the dark cellar.

The wind outside quieted. We climbed out to take a peek. Things were blown over, but the buildings were still standing. Aunt Grace insisted I stay longer. "It wouldn't be good if you was on the road and the cloud decided to return." After an hour I started home.

When I arrived, Mama was as white as a sheet hanging on the line. She ran toward me with outstretched arms and gave me a big hug. Seventeen years old and it was the first time my mama had hugged me! "Thank God, you're safe," she said. Then as if nothing had happened, she returned to the kitchen to finish supper. I stood there thinking, "How nice that greeting felt." The warmth of expressed love covered me from top to bottom. I didn't want to move and break the spell.

Papa arrived about two hours later. Mama repeated the hug and then, as if embarrassed by her show of affection, she backed away, looking at Papa's grim face. "Bad news," he shook his head. "The Sheldons are gone."

"What?" Mama and I gasped at the same time. "They've only been here nine months," Mama cried. "What happened?"

Papa was in town when the cloud hit. "Sheldons' neighbors down in the valley rode to town to get help. They heard an explosion and saw things flying through the air as they headed for their root cellar. When it got quiet, they ran up the hill. Nothin' was left of the Sheldons' house except the basement with an untouched box of goose feathers in the corner. They searched the farm. Found Albert in the manure pile behind the barn and Rachel hanging from a tree. Neither survived. There was straw driven clean through tree limbs and trunks. Boards were everywhere like the house exploded from the inside out. The barn and animals were hurt at all."

What kind of horrible storm was this? God, how could you allow such a thing? Inside, I began to scream at God. I was fearful. I was angry. I was resentful. I was confused.

"Odd thing," Papa was saying, "they moved out here from Kansas to get away from twisters. Seems like that scripture in Ecclesiastes is proven true—'It's appointed unto man once to die.' Almost like God was saying you can run, but you can't get away from me."

For months, people were finding pieces of the house, furniture, and clothes for miles around. I still questioned God. I found the courage one day to ask Grandma Kole how God could allow such a thing to happen. Her loving grandma arms wrapped around me as she said, "Susan, we don't know. God's the one who knows everything. He sees the future, He knows the past. Just like the Bible says, it's a broken world with hard things in it. We can't fix it. We can only trust God to make us stronger so we can live through the storms."

I knew Grandma was right. She'd lived in hard times beyond her control. Her faith was a strong example. She prayed with me as I asked God to forgive me for doubting Him. Then we sang, "This world is not my home, I'm just a passin' through. My treasures are laid up somewhere beyond the blue." My goal was heaven. Whatever I had to live through here wasn't important. He was making a place for me to live forever. It was going to be perfect.

Chapter 18

It Happened One Summer

Johnny hated farming. He kept looking for other work—easy, quick moneymakers. He tried selling McNess. The folks gave him money for the initial stock of drink mixes, pie fillings, and spices. He hadn't sold the entire first supply before he was off on another adventure. He'd rather party than work. He bought a motorcycle with the McNess profits and never returned the initial investment. Time after time, he borrowed money from Mama and Papa for a new scheme. It drained the resources Papa needed to replant and run the farm. I could sense the disappointment of my folks who couldn't say no to their only son. I vowed I would never be that kind of burden to them.

When I turned eighteen, Mama gave me a lecture. "Susan, you're more than a woman now. Don't be old like me when you have children. It's too hard. Get to thinking about marriage. There are young men available around here now, but if you wait too long, they'll all be married and you'll have to take some man no one else wanted."

Oh. That had never occurred to me. I knew all the young men around here and not a single one of them would I want to spend the rest of my life with—especially Walt. What was I going to do? I'd have to pray about this.

The next morning I had a thought. *Uncle Jim had found Aunt Grace in another town. Maybe that's what I should do, look for someone that lived some other place. I liked Aunt Grace a lot. There had to be marriageable men out there, too.*

Shortly before my eighteenth birthday, Mama sent me to Aunt Grace's with some strawberries from the day's picking. When I arrived, a strange car sat in front of the house. Cars were still rare on the Camas Prairie, but were accepted as a means of travel. Even Mama allowed herself a ride in Papa and Johnny's. Can you believe she even rode on Johnny's motorcycle? This was the lady that made us come in when she heard a car a half mile away! She was so hard to understand sometimes.

No one ever knocked in those days, and family always used the kitchen door. "Hello," I called to the voices coming from the living room. "I brought some strawberries."

"Come on in," Grace invited. "Got someone I want you to meet."

As I rounded the corner from the kitchen, my breath was taken away by a young man sitting across from Aunt Grace. "Susan, this is my brother, Tom. He's come to help on the farm this summer. He'll be staying a few months."

"I'm pleased to meet you, Tom," I responded. "I like your sister. Nice to have you visiting or should I say working here?"

Tom stood. He was very tall. I had to look up to notice his hazel eyes that sparkled under dark eyebrows and wavy black hair. *Good looking,* I thought. *Polite. Stood when he was introduced.* "Oh, I'm sorry what did you say?" I suddenly realized he'd been talking.

"It's good to meet you. I've heard a lot about you from my sister. She says you're a good cook and can clean a house faster than a tornado."

I quickly looked at Aunt Grace who just shrugged her shoulders and said, "It's just an expression, Susan." My impression of a tornado was not positive after the one that hit our community just a year ago. My mind flashed back to that awful day of destruction.

"Did I say something wrong?" Tom asked.

"Tornados aren't too well liked around here. We had one a year ago that killed a young couple," I replied.

"Sorry, didn't mean to stir up bad memories."

I sat and visited. Grace excused herself to start supper. Left alone, it was a bit awkward. What should I ask? What do I tell a young man I've just met? I was smitten with those golden eyes and the rugged jaw. He talked about farming, how he liked to feel the dirt and smell of things growing. He hoped to have a farm of his own someday. I learned he was my senior by five years. Wouldn't Avis be amazed? He worked most of the time on his father's and neighbors' farms at Clearwater, but he wanted to strike out on his own. He had no definite plans, except to go to Lewiston where he could get on at the new mill.

It was getting late, and I needed to get home before supper. I excused myself with, "Mama will be needing help with supper. I'd better go."

"Well, can't have a pretty lady walking home by herself," Tom exclaimed. "Do you mind if I walk you home?"

What could I say? So he walked me home that day, the next day, and the next, and many days after that.

He came to our farm to help with harvest when the threshing machine arrived. Just like before, all farmers came to gather the grain, sew bags, and haul it into town. Grace came to help Mama in the kitchen, and they kept me busy taking water out to the field for the workers. I had no idea there was a plan going on between them. I was excited to be in the field so I could see Tom. There was something about him that made my heart do flip-flops.

At the end of August, we were working Uncle Jim's farm. Again, I was the chosen water carrier who also rang the dinner bell, calling them at one o'clock to come eat. I knew Tom was tired. I could tell by the way he walked. When he saw me, his face would light up with a smile; he'd tip his hat at me. I found my heart jumping. I found any excuse I could to go into the field.

Two more fields and harvest was finished. There had been several days at other farms when I stayed with Edna while Mama went to help. My heart ached to see Tom. "Thomas Albert," I said to myself. "I think I could spend the rest of my life with you." I never told anyone. I forced my mind to take over my emotions, hoping and praying no one suspected I might like this man. Looking back, I doubt very much if I covered it up.

Life slowed with harvest winding down. Each farmer retreated to his own place, analyzing crop figures, cleaning equipment, and making sure enough seed was saved for the spring planting.

The twelfth of September, Tom was walking me home from Aunt Grace and Uncle Jim's when he stopped abruptly. I had walked on a few steps before I realized he wasn't beside me. I turned. "Susan," he said as he walked up to me, "I think I've walked you home enough." My heart sank. "Susan, I . . . uh . . . I don't want to walk you home any more—except to walk you to our home. Will you marry me?" My heart leaped into my mouth. I was speechless. His face looked worried.

I was worried because I couldn't talk. How could this have happened in only three months?

I found my voice. "Yes . . . yes . . . I would like to marry you, but . . . but you'll have to ask Papa for his permission." Our faces broke into wide smiles. He reached out and took my hand. Oh my, I thought, this is the first time he's even touched me. How proper and considerate he is. He'll be the perfect husband. I dreamed the rest of the way home about a perfect marriage, a perfect home, surrounded by perfect kids.

We made a mad dash to my house, took a deep breath, and opened the squeaky screen door. I hurried upstairs and left Tom with Papa and Mama. I could hear the sound of his voice and Papa responding. I prayed Papa would say yes. What would I do if he said no?

Mama knocked on my door, and her stern voice echoed in the hall. "Susan, we want to talk to you." They don't like him. They're going to say no. She turned and went back down the stairs. I held my breath and followed.

"Susan," Papa began, "this young man says he wants to marry you and asked my permission. What do you think about that?"

"I . . . I . . . I think it would be good." I stuttered. I didn't dare look at Tom. I had no idea what Papa's answer was.

"You haven't known him very long. Remember, marriage is for life," Papa reminded.

"I know, Papa. We've had lots of time to talk when he's walked me home. I think he will be a fine husband for me." I glanced at Tom and blushed.

"Well, you have your mother's and my permission to get married." Papa smiled.

"Oh, Papa." I cried throwing my arms around him. "Thank you."

Mama, who had been sitting quietly, now was all business. "Susan, Tom says he has to be in Lewiston on the twelfth of October for a job that's waiting him. That means we only have a short time to plan a wedding. Your uncle can perform the ceremony, your grandmama can sew your dress, and I'll make a cake. Do you mind if it's just family?"

"Oh please, could Avis come too?"

Chapter 19

A Trip to the City

October 11, 1928. The date was set. Just four weeks to put a wedding together! I didn't want anything fancy. I never liked being the center of attention. I was so "in love" I didn't realize everything was revolving around me.

Grandmama began sewing immediately. I had my secret, "wedding-dreaming eyes" set on the white satin and French lace at the Reubens general store for a long time. I wanted flapper style with an overdress of white lace tied with a satin belt around the hips. It only needed three measurements—bust, shoulders, and length (which would hit two inches above the knees).

Shoes? Now that was a problem. To order them from the catalogue would take too long. Mama, Papa, and I trekked off to the city of Lewiston to find a pair of white pumps. "Sorry," the clerk said. "It's the wrong time of year for white. How about a lovely pair in black satin?"

"Mercy no," Mama cried. "This is for a wedding. They have to be white." My mama was standing up for me? Insisting I have the right shoes? Talking back to a stranger? Like the one-time hug, I felt temporarily loved.

The shop owner came out to see what the fuss was. "Can I help?" he asked.

Mama quickly explained the problem. The man scratched his head and disappeared behind a curtain into the back room. We waited. Had he forgotten us? We were about to leave when he emerged holding a pair of white pumps. "Let's see if these will fit. I put them in storage after they didn't sell last summer."

I sat in a chair and removed my Mary Janes. "Of course you'll need to have silk stockings to wear with these," he continued. "Just a minute." Again he disappeared behind the curtain. He returned holding a pair of long, tan, transparent stockings. Never saw anything like them. "Now you must be very careful when you put these on. If you snag the silk, they will run and that doesn't look pretty." Run? I had no idea what that meant. Silk? How much did they cost? I looked at Mama and Papa with questioning eyes. Papa nodded. Very carefully I put the fine hose on the foot I'd burned with hot coffee. Even after two years, it was still red, tender, and sensitive to the touch of a shoe. I held my breath. It had to fit. It just had to. I couldn't go barefoot at my wedding. He took the shoe and expertly slipped it on my foot. Just like the prince with the glass slipper, it was a perfect fit. My prince, Tom, was waiting for me on a farm just outside Reubens. I felt like a queen.

The salesman carefully wrapped the precious stockings and shoes in separate tissue papers, tied them with a string, and I slipped them into my bag. Papa gave him a large bill plus some silver dollars. He never told me how much. He said, "It's a gift from my heart."

"Let's eat lunch at the little cafe next door." Papa suggested. White shoes, silk stockings, and lunch in a cafe! It was the best day of my life. Well, not the best, but it ranked close to the top.

"I'd like a hotdog, Papa." Mama looked at me and wrinkled up her nose. She called them store-made meat, not fit for eating. "I love hotdogs. Could I have ice cream too?" Mama nodded her head. We had ice cream about twice a year. When Papa broke the ice on the pond and brought big chunks to pack in the sawdust of the underground ice cellar, we'd save out some of the small pieces to make ice cream. Never had any of the fancy flavors though until Johnny started selling McNess. By the time the ice on the pond was gone, the ice cellar was still cool enough to safely store strawberry pickings and make strawberry ice cream.

In 1928, Lewiston was a busy place with a port, a railroad line, and a large new pine mill. That's where Tom had his new job. I was all eyes and ears. This was going to be my new home. So many people, so many cars, so much noise—it was exciting! I knew I was going to love it. I also understood that this country girl was looking at big changes in her life.

We ambled up and down the streets of the big city. Being it was a Saturday and past harvest, we ran into people we knew from all over the prairie. Of course, we had to stop and talk. Catching up on the news was the best part of going to any town. Mama and Papa had to spread the news about their daughter getting married. After repeating it at least ten times, the reality of what I was about to do started to sink in. *What am I getting myself into?*

Chapter 20

What About Edna?

Time flew with much to do. Tom went to Lewiston to find a place for us to live. Mama and I scrubbed the house from top to bottom. Our house wasn't as big as either of the grandparents', but you were expected to get married in your folks' house. We moved most of the furniture out of the sitting room and set up board benches and dining room chairs. Remember, our family would total in the sixties if they all came. Some of my cousins were getting married so that number was rising. Some people were going to have to stand. Good thing it wasn't going to be a long ceremony. I did get to invite Avis, but she couldn't come. She was in bed with morning sickness. They were going to have a baby!

It hit my little sister the hardest. "Who's gonna take care of me? Who's gonna help me with my homework? Who's gonna teach me how to embroider and sew? Who's gonna push me in the swing?" She hounded my steps, bombarding me with question upon question. Every waking moment when not in school, she kept me in her sight. She was ten years old, smart and talented. She wrote great stories and had exceptional artistic talent. One time, she was required to draw the state of Idaho, filling in the main cities and where we lived. Her map was so perfect that the teacher thought she had traced it and tore it up. Mama heard the teacher discussing it on the party line with another parent and immediately pulled her out of school.

"I'm gonna miss you so much," she said a hundred times a day as she tagged after me. "Can I come live with you? Why do you have to move so far away? Please, please, please stay here with me; don't go with Tom."

How was I going to leave my Edna? For ten years she had been the purpose of my life. She had loved me unconditionally. I hadn't carried her in my body, but she had been the one who kept me steady, giving me the joy of a real purpose in life. I promised over and over, "You can come visit any time. I'll come and visit you too. We'll have new things to share with each other." Heaps of guilt for abandoning her gnawed at my heart.

The day before the wedding, Edna and I sat on the front porch weaving daisy chains. Even though it was feeling like fall, wild daisies still covered the fields. We had gone out early in the morning and picked buckets of them. "Edna, would you like to be my flower girl?"

"Do I get to be in the wedding?" she questioned.

I smiled and thought, It's important is for her to have good memories of today. "Yes, you will have the important job of throwing flowers in front of me as Papa walks me down to Tom and Uncle Willie."

"I know what flowers I'll use," she exclaimed. "It'll be a secret." I was curious but wanted to let her surprise me.

Three hours later the sitting room was draped in pink and white daisy chains. At the far end of the room sat two bouquets of pink and white roses.

Come October 11, Mama spent the morning making applesauce cake, my favorite. It would be served with a drizzle of applesauce over each piece and a big dab of whipped cream on top. The cold drink was made from the leftover McNess fruit punch Johnny sold. The coffee had been perked and was keeping warm on the back of the wood stove in a big metal pot. Even though the wedding wouldn't start two o'clock, people started coming a little after noon. Grandparents were the first to arrive so they could lend a hand. Of course Uncle Willie was there to do his preacher duties and pray for us. But there was no Tom. I tried hard not to think about the possibility he might change his mind or maybe he had an accident coming back from Lewiston.

Upstairs, sitting in white satin and lace I felt beautiful, but extremely nervous. I looked around my room. My life would never be the same after today. The room was bare. The precious few things I called my own were packed in a box and a small suitcase, ready for the trip to Lewiston soon after the wedding. These plain wooden walls held memories of tears, sickness, and sadness. Good things too: cousins piled into the room to chatter or stay all night and Edna coming to snuggle in my bed. Wishes and dreams had been born in this small space. The best times? It was here that I learned how to talk to God. It was here I grew as His child. *God, go with me no matter where I go. I don't know where that's going to be. I've just gotta trust you.*

Do not be afraid. I'll go with you, echoed the words I had read. A knock on the door brought me back. I opened it and found Aunt Grace looking fretful. "I think something's happened to Tom. He's not come yet. I sent Jim looking for him."

There was a sharp twist in my stomach. It threatened to upheave the food that I had forgotten to eat. "What time is it?" I asked.

"It's two fifteen. It's not like him to be late. I'll let you know when he gets here. Meanwhile, you pray." Aunt Grace closed the door. I listened to her heavy shoes clomping down the stairs.

What could I do but pray? I sat on the bed near tears and started talking to God. *Where is he, God? Where's my Tom? This was going to be the best day of my life. Now, I don't even know where he is. If something's happened to him, I'll never come out of my room again. God, please get him here safely.*

Cast all your cares on Me. I care for you. I dabbed my eyes and prayed in earnest for the man I was about to marry. Twenty minutes later another knock came.

"He's here," Aunt Grace announced. "He had a flat tire." She hurried back down stairs. I heard the scrape of chairs and voices quieting below. Uncle Willie wound up the phonograph and placed the needle on the recording of the wedding march. Again chairs moved as people stood. I made my way down the stairs, took Papa's arm, and stepped into the crowded room ready to begin my new life.

Daisy chains lined the walls, the rose bouquets were beautiful; when I looked down at Edna walking in front of us, I laughed out loud. My flower girl was throwing dandelions on everyone in the crowd.

Tom and his best friend, Wendell Kleinsmith, stood between the rose bouquets, next to Uncle Willie. He looked handsome in his brown suit and tan tie in spite of the smudge of dirt on his cheek. There was a frown on his face until he saw me; it turned upside down and his eyes twinkled. At last it was all coming together. We would soon be pronounced Mr. and Mrs. Thomas Albert Chase.

Chapter 21

A New Beginning

It was eight o'clock before Tom and I began pulling ourselves away from the hugs and goodbyes. There were tears of joy and tears of sadness. Papa's eyes welled up as he gave me a hug and said, "Don't be a stranger, but remember you belong with your husband now."

That's when I couldn't keep it in any longer. Tears dripped from my nose and chin with small sobs rising from my throat. My champion, my support, my papa. I'd never been away from him more than twenty-four hours. *How could I live without my papa to listen to my heart?*

As if he had heard my thoughts, he continued, "You'll learn to share your heart with Tom. He'll be your hero. Close the Kole book. Your Mrs. Chase book will have new characters with us woven in here and there. We'll always love you, but can't go with you. God will always love you and will always be with you." With that he kissed my forehead as he had so many times in my life to soothe my hurts and turned to hand me off to Tom.

As I took Tom's arm, we were violently pushed apart by my angry, blond ten-year-old sister. "No!" she yelled. The room hushed. "No, you can't take my Susie. She's my sister. She belongs to me." She threw her arms around me like a vise. I looked at Tom. It was getting late. I was torn. What could I do? I started rubbing her back like every time she was upset and began to sing, "Hush little baby don't say a word . . ." The words were broken with sobs from both of us. She relaxed into my arms. "We'll see each other again soon. I promise." She nodded. "One last hug?"

The three-hour ride began in silence. I sat looking out the window at nothing because it was already dark. Driving at night on country roads was hazardous. Cattle wander at will, deer cross the road going to the creek, coyotes chase rabbits who waited too long to run to their holes. I felt like Alice, falling into my hole, following the magic white rabbit of my dreams. I had dreamed big, perfect, amazing dreams. Now I was facing real life. I was nervous. Downright scared. What had I gotten myself into?

I glanced over at my husband. Husband? How strange to called Tom my husband? *Husband. Husband.* I repeated it over and over, trying to convince myself that this was real. It was moonlit enough to see his handsome face, set and serious. *What do you suppose he's thinking? I asked myself. Is he as scared as I am?*

I took a deep breath and tried to find my voice, "I'm sorry . . . about Edna. She did good during the ceremony. It's hard on her, you know. I've taken care of her more than Mama. I'm going to miss her so much."

We rode on in outstretched silence. Tom finally said, "You're gonna be a good mama."

We finally hit pavement. It was safer, but still only wide enough for two cars. At night, few cars were on the road. The car lights didn't shine far. Tom wasn't familiar with this route to Lewiston so he drove slower than usual, making sure he saw the curves ahead. He finally spoke again, "Found us a house in Clarkston. Sits on a corner, doesn't have much yard. It's white with green trim. Has running water inside, an outhouse close in the back. No furniture yet except a bed." My head jerked toward him then quickly straight ahead. Horror, fear, and embarrassment flooded my mind. A bed? I was going to get in a bed with a man? My dreams hadn't included that part of the "perfect" life. What have I gotten myself into?

We arrived in Clarkston after midnight. The back seat of our car was full of gifts from family and supplies from Papa and Mama to help us get started. The quiet after the long ride was deafening. Tom opened my door, and together we walked up to the house on the corner of Eleventh and Bridge Street. He opened the door and lit a match to find the oil lamp on the kitchen counter. Bright light filled the house, giving it an immense look. Our shadows filled the living room walls.

"Wait here," Tom spoke softly, "I'll go get our bags."

While waiting I took a step. The floors creaked. Sounded like home. It had that same "lived in" kind of smell. It needed some calcimine on the walls, but it wasn't bad.

Tom returned with my suitcase and his bag. "You carry the light." He led the way to the back room where the bed stood against the wall. "I'll sleep on the outside. I have to be to work at 7:00 in the morning. You won't have to get up. I'll put things from the car in the house before I leave. You can put 'em away tomorrow." With that he began to pull off his clothes down to his undies. I quickly turned my back, opened my little suitcase, pulled out my warm gown, and slipped into the other room to put it on. Exhaustion overcame us as soon as we hit the lumpy, cold bed.

I never heard him leave in the morning. I woke to the sun shining on my face and total silence except for the occasional car passing. "I'm alone," I thought. "I don't know a soul in this place, except Tom. I'm utterly alone."

I was suddenly impressed with how fortunate I had been to have Papa, Mama, Edna, and yes, even Johnny, all my life. The quiet shouted at me, but I heard a whisper in my mind, *I'll never leave you nor forsake you.* "Thank you, Jesus," I whispered back.

Chapter 22

Meeting the Family

My first week as Mrs. T. A. Chase was busy with cleaning, putting my own ideas into the house, making sure my husband had a hot breakfast, food in his lunchpail, a good supper, and clean clothes. That's what a good wife does.

The area was new to both of us. We only had each other for company. Which is just fine when you're a newlywed. We were in love, but I found myself guarded and private as always. I couldn't share much with this man I'd only known three months. Would he understand? I kept safe by keeping silent. Tom, although I knew he loved me, was also quiet about anything intimate. Down deep, I think he was also a shy, private person. Two private people trying to become one in marriage; we lived on the edge of questions we were afraid to ask.

I have to admit I was homesick. I missed my papa most of all. He was the one who wisely listened to my thoughts and gave me his understanding heart. My little sister? How could I desert her? My mind still heard her cries as we were about to leave. She depended on me for the first ten years of her life. Who was going to take care of her now I was gone? I was full of guilt and failure. My mind whirled all day long with questions, arguments, and doubts. The biggest of all? Could this man I married ever understand and care about me like Papa and Edna?

I made a resolution. I guess back in that day you'd have called it a promise—a promise to myself and to Tom, although I never shared it with him. I was going to be a perfect wife. Everything I did would be done to please my husband so he would love me like I longed to be loved. I would do all he asked me to do. I would be what he expected me to be. I would never complain. I was letting myself fall back into the same trap of wanting to please Mama, only this time it was my husband. It seemed right and comfortable. I knew how to do this.

Tom had to be at work at seven o'clock every morning so we were always in bed by eight-thirty and up at five-thirty. Ten days passed. We were getting into a routine. We had gone to bed. Tom was already asleep. He worked hard pulling the logs into the sawmill. As I was slowly winding down and drifting into sleep, I heard a scuffling sound on the front porch. I sat up, my heart pounding. Tom didn't hear. He snored on. There were voices and sounds of footsteps outside. Not ever having lived in a city, I froze with fear. What should I do? Should I wake my tired husband and risk him being angry with me? Should I crawl over him and go look out the window? Where was that shotgun he'd told me about?

I didn't have to make the decision. The air was suddenly filled with horns, banging pots and pans, lights, yelling, and things rattling. That brought Tom out of his deep sleep. Jumping out of bed, he grabbed his pants and stumbled into the living room trying to put them on. I cried out, "No, Tom—be careful." I tore after him in my long flannel nightgown.

"Oh, no! I should have known!" he yelled. Then he began laughing.

"Known what? What's going on?" I screeched above the noise, which now included banging on the door.

"It's my family!" he shouted.

"Your family? This is your family?" I was mortified. The only member of his family I knew was Aunt Grace. The rest of the family hadn't even come to the wedding. What were they doing here in our front yard making all this racket? What kind of family did I marry into? Are they all crazy? I suddenly became aware that I was standing there in nothing but my nightgown. I rushed into the bedroom and grabbed my robe. "How can I meet his family looking like this," I thought as I used my fingers to push my hair in place.

Tom opened the door and his brothers, sisters, aunts, uncles, cousins, and mother and father came spilling into the house, still banging, tooting horns and singing, "If you knew Susie like I knew Susie. . . "

Oh if they only knew how much I hated that song. I hoped my face didn't show my feelings.

They certainly seemed to be having a grand time. They were laughing, slapping Tom on the back, and filling our small kitchen counter with piles of food. Grace was the first to reach me outside the bedroom door. She gave me a hug and shouted in my ear, "It's okay, Susie. This is your chivaree. Welcome to the family." I had never heard of a chivaree. I guess my Dutch/Irish ancestry was too reserved for such carrying on. Grace explained, "Family and friends throw a surprise party for the newlywed couple just when they least expect it to celebrate their union. Were you surprised?"

Surprised? Was I ever! Scared, surprised, humiliated, and very uncomfortable. I said in Tom's ear, "I'm going to get dressed." He nodded and I retreated to the bedroom. I dressed as fast as I could.

Suddenly the doorknob rattled and my heart was again in my throat. Who could it be? "Susie, I'm coming in. Are ya ready for me?" I just needed to put on my shoes. Who was this? Who would dare enter my bedroom? Why didn't Tom see this happening? He knew where I was.

I opened the door. There was a gray-haired man leaning against the hall wall, grinning from ear to ear. Not a good grin, more a leer. "Betcha I scared the bejesus out of ya. Ah, come on pretty girl, don't look so scared. I was only teasing." I slipped past his outreached hand and ran to find Tom among the many bodies crammed into the house. I never left his side the rest of the night.

Tom began introducing me. There were two other sisters, Neva and Frankie. Frankie? Yes, I remembered when my brother dated her. Didn't get to know her well. Johnny never brought her to the house except for a couple of dances. She was beautiful with pale skin and dark wavy hair. She gave me a hug and said, "Welcome to the family, Susie."

Neva was older. She wore her hair pulled straight back and in a bun on top of her head. She gave my arm a squeeze. "I think Tom's found a good wife." She smiled. "Very pretty." She had deep brown eyes, a sharp contrast to Frankie and Grace's blue and Tom's hazel.

We continued threading our way through. There were three brothers: Irvin, Stanley, and Paris. Paris was the youngest, only nine years old, a skinny boy with unruly dark hair and a crooked grin. He immediately captured my heart.

Finally, we reached the corner where our only chair sat in the living room. Perched on it was a tiny lady who Tom introduced as his mother, Lilly. She looked small and frail, not at all like a farm wife. Tom said she could work from dawn till dark with the rest of them. You could see his deep love for her in his eyes as he introduced me. When she smiled, I felt like someone lit a new lamp. She was beautiful even with her white hair and wrinkled face.

A man stepped next to her and commanded, "It's time ya introduce your father, Tom. I've been made to wait way too long." I instinctively stepped back. It was the voice at the bedroom door. I gathered courage to put on a smile, looked up, and responded, "Pleased to meet you," and shook his hand. He grabbed my hand and pulled me hard to him, knocking the air from me. My pleading eyes went to my husband. He simply said, "Father likes girls" and turned away.

Chapter 23

The Silence

A little past midnight the last reveler left. The house was deathly quiet. Tom didn't say a word. He went to the kitchen sink, washed up a bit, and disappeared into the bedroom. Homesickness, exhaustion, nervousness from meeting the family and enduring my advancing father-in-law left me in a puddle of tears.

Where was my husband? He should be here to comfort me and listen like Papa always did. When I finally controlled my sobs, I heard Tom snoring through the bedroom door.

My heart was torn in two. Lonely and abandoned, I fell to my knees in front of our only chair and cried, "Oh, God. How can I do this? I hurt so bad. No one cares. I'm alone, I'm afraid."

I will never leave you, or forsake you. Do not be afraid.

"Yes, I know you said that. It's good you said it, but I don't think I can believe it. I'm in a horrible place. I don't feel you. I don't feel anything. I'm numb. I can't even think. I want to escape."

Trust in me with all your heart and lean not on your own understanding, acknowledge me and I will direct your paths.

"Trust?" I replied bitterly, "I trusted my husband and what did I get? Nothing! Not even protection. At least Papa would come to my rescue. This man snoring in the other room doesn't love me or even care what happens to me. He just wants to sleep . . ."

I don't know how long I argued and complained to God about my predicament. The next thing I knew Tom was shaking my shoulder and saying, "It's six-thirty." He walked out slamming the door.

"What? No! Oh no! Your lunch . . . I didn't get to make you . . . a lunch . . . or breakfast or . . ." My voice trailed off as I heard the car start then leave. Tears flooded my eyes again. How can one person have so many tears?

I pushed myself off the bare wood floor. "Ouch," I cried as my hand was attacked by a big splinter. "Now that just adds injury to insult," I complained out loud. "Oh, well it's not the first time." I went to find a needle. I held it in the flame of the lamp Tom had lit to make his lunch. "It has to be sterilized before you dig in after a piece of wood." Papa always said. It was deep. I could do this. It was in the side of my right hand and try as I might, I couldn't make my left hand prick, pry, or push that sliver out. Exasperated, I finally gave up.

"Now what?" I asked myself. The sliver distraction had brought me back to the reality of the messy house. People had flooded in, eaten, drunk, and flooded out, leaving a disaster.

"Where should I start? The least messy room. The bedroom." I didn't want to go there. My last time there held scary memories—changing, pounding on the door, a leering old man. Did that really happen? I forced myself to quickly open the door, make the bed and leave. I didn't realize I'd been holding my breath until I reached the living room. I picked up cups, glasses, pieces of food, and dirty plates stacking them in the kitchen. I grabbed the broom and swept with all my might. Then filling a bucket, I scrubbed that floor for all I was worth—trying to wash last night out of the house. I stood in the kitchen looking at the clean room. It still dug deep in my memory. I could see my father-in-law standing by the chair, grinning. I tiptoed across the wet floor, grabbed the chair, and turned it around to face the corner. Now for the kitchen.

It was good—cleaning, washing, sweeping, mopping. The house sparkled, but I was hot, sweating, and needing a bath. No time. I took a quick sponge bath and started supper. I had failed miserably as a wife this morning. I would make a great supper. Tom's family had brought a big ham. Lots of meat was left on the bone. Ham and navy beans had always been my favorite. I stoked up the wood stove that had burned low all day and put on the pot. Too bad I didn't get some fresh bread started rising this morning. The dried-out bread from Tuesday's baking could soak up the soup.

Two hours later, I heard Tom's car pull in the driveway. I knew he was going to be tired. I would try hard to make his evening relaxing and enjoyable. I smoothed my apron and put on my best smile, glanced at the already set supper table and gave the beans one last stir. The door opened. I ran over and gave him a hug and asked about his day. I chattered on about cleaning and filled a big bowl for each of us. It wasn't until I sat down to eat I realized Tom hadn't said a word. Silence hung heavy over our meal. I had put aside my tears that morning and concentrated on making a good finish to the day. My husband had retreated somewhere inside and refused to come out. I was confused. Was this my fault? What had I done? Is he blaming me for his father's behavior? Why won't he talk to me?

How do I break this ice that's growing between us after only one week of marriage? Maybe if I just carry on the conversation, he'll eventually talk to me. "I can't imagine how tired you were today at work after only five hours sleep. I have a hard time even thinking when I don't get enough sleep. If I get up and move around, then I'm better, but give me a book and I'll soon be nodding . . ." Scrape! Tom scooted his chair back, stood, looked at me, and walked out of the kitchen. *Oh, dear. That didn't go well. I'll just have to try harder.* I began to clear the table. Tears were on the brink of exploding again.

By the time I finished washing the dishes and putting food away, I could hear Tom snoring in the bedroom. After turning off the kerosene lamp, I crawled over the end of the bed carefully into my place next to the wall.

The next morning I bounded out to get Tom's breakfast and make his lunch before he went out the door. The silent treatment still met me. I made no attempt at conversation. You can only carry on a one-sided conversation so long.

It was the same, day after day. Time moved like a snail. I was hungry for conversation. Yet, I was becoming somewhat comfortable in the quiet aloneness, even when I was with him. I had so many questions, but kept them to myself because I knew he wouldn't answer. So during the day I talked out loud to myself and to God.

The memory of the chivaree began to fade like a bad dream. I struggled to keep my eyes on what needed to be done. On the seventh day, I walked across the bridge to the hardware store in Lewiston and bought some blue calcimine. Before Tom arrived home that evening, I had painted the living room and hall.

I just finished cleaning the brush when my husband drove in. I hid around the corner in the table end of the kitchen and held my breath. How was he going to react? Will he say anything? Will he even notice? Heavy footsteps clunked up the front steps and stopped on the porch. He always took off his boots before coming in to keep mud and sawdust out of the house. I heard him brushing off his coat. I was shaking with suspense. The doorknob turned and he stepped in. Silence.

I heard him stocking foot it down to the bedroom then come back. "Would you look at that!" he exclaimed. Suddenly he and I were nose to nose as he peeked around the short wall where I was hiding. "It's beautiful, Susie." He wrapped me in a bear hug then kissed me. "It sure makes the place look different. Now I'm thinking we need to start looking for a second-hand davenport so more than one person can sit and admire these purdy blue walls . . ." He continued to chatter on and on about anything and everything that had happened during the last silent week.

I had my Tom back.

Chapter 24

The Dress

During the next two weeks, we managed to get into a routine. During Tom's days off, he would drive me around the area to see the sights of the valley. It was a great geography lesson. On one side of the Snake River was the biggest town called Lewiston, Idaho. It had the mill where many people worked and a long main street with a variety of stores. On our side of the Snake River was a small community called Clarkston. It was in the state of Washington. These two towns were connected by a wooden bridge with trolley tracks running between the two lanes.

One day I braved getting on the trolley and rode all the way to the end of Lewiston's main street. I brought a shopping bag but didn't have much money so I looked. So many, many beautiful things! I was amazed at the jewelry, the furniture, the store-made dresses. Store-made dresses? I never had a store-made dress. Oh, how fine they were. My heart longed for one. If only I had enough money to buy one. No, I could not spend Tom's hard-earned money on something I didn't need. What a waste that would be! I had plenty of clothes. Who needs more than three dresses? One for going to church, one to do housework, and the third to wear for shopping and visiting.

My curiosity drew me from the display window into the store. There were many dresses to choose from, along with racks of coats, petticoats, underclothes, shirtwaists, and skirts. Then I spotted it. Made from a silky navy blue material, it fell straight from the shoulders to just above the knees where it was completed by six inches of pleats. Never had I been so captured by a piece of clothing.

"May I help you find a dress?" asked the clerk who I hadn't seen come up next to me.

"Uh, no thank you. I'm . . . just looking right now." I wasn't sure if I said the right thing. I'd never been in a store like this before.

The lady smiled, "If you'd like to try on something, please let me know." Try it on? Right here in the store. I felt a surge of embarrassment. How could I try on a dress with everyone watching? Even when Grandmama had sewn my dresses, I always went into one of the bedrooms to put it on for the fitting. I dashed out of the store.

I continued walking along Main Street. My mind wandered to the store clothes, my clothes, my future clothes. Hmm. This was something I hadn't considered before I got married. I didn't have Mama or Grandmama to make my clothes now. What would happen when my clothes wore out? I would have to get them in a store. I didn't have a sewing machine. I could mend by hand. Yes, I would mend and patch both my and Tom's clothes. I would keep us neat and clean. That's respectable and proper.

Time? What time is it? How long had I been wandering around gawking? I looked up at the large clock in front of the jewelry store. Three o'clock. Oh, dear, I've got to get home. It's time to get dinner started. How do I get back on the trolley? How do I get it to stop? I heard its rumble. It was going the other direction! How long would it take to go to the end and come back? Could I run back to the end of the line in time to get on? I doubted it. I had to find out. I dashed into the jewelry store and looked frantically for help. A man with a strange glass eye looked up. "May I show you something?" he asked.

"Yes, please show me where to catch the trolley to Clarkston." I blurted out. "I must catch the next run."

"You're right where you need to be," he assured me. "The trolley stops right in front of our shop."

"Thank you!" I shouted, and headed out the door.

"Wait," he called after me, but I was already out the door. He followed me out with a ticket in his hand. "You didn't get a ticket. It's five cents." He thrust it toward me. I dug out my coin purse and handed him a nickel. Blushing, I thanked him. "Happy to help, young lady."

Only an hour to get dinner. From the Clarkston stop, I ran un-lady-like the six blocks to our house, threw open the door, tossed my coat and hat on the chair, and headed for the kitchen. Kole hash, I had decided. That means you throw whatever's in the kitchen into the frying pan, get it warm, then make gravy to go over the top of it: leftover potatoes from last night, an onion, a few carrots, and a small piece of beef roast left from our Sunday dinner and crumbled-up dry bread to stretch it.

I had been in such a hurry I didn't put on my apron. I stoked up the fire with kindling to get it burning faster. Suddenly the pitchy wood snapped, throwing a spark at me. I slammed the door. Too late. There was a brown, burned spot on the front of my going-to-town dress. If only I had taken the time to put my apron on!

I shoved the food on the back of the stove and hurried into the bedroom to change into my housedress and put on my apron. "Foolish woman," I chided myself. "Don't ever forget to put your apron on in the house." As I rolled up my town dress, the brown spot crumbled in my hands. I hid it. I would have to think about this problem later. My husband must come first. I was setting the table when Tom came home.

He gave me a kiss and hug, lifted the lid to the fry pan, and stared at me. "What is this?" he almost whispered.

"It's Kole hash," I whispered back. We both laughed and sat down to eat. Milk! I had forgotten to get milk in town. That was the only thing I planned to buy. Tom always liked milk with his dinner. I humbly apologized. "I guess we'll have to drink water."

Not only had I wasted hours looking at pretties, but I failed again to be the perfect wife. Another lesson learned. Don't get sidetracked. Think, think, think. You must be the perfect wife so your husband will love you.

Chapter 25

A Call Home

The fourth weekend of our marriage, Tom came in all excited. "Great news!" he shouted. "My cousins, Curtis and Charlie, are movin' into the house right behind us on Bridge Street."

"Uh, have I met them?" I faltered, trying hard to remember those names from that horrible night of meeting his family.

"No, no. They've been living in Mexico." He was grinning from ear to ear. "Their Dad died so they came back here to live."

"Mexico! That's another country. What in the world were they doing there?" I couldn't believe anyone would want to live any place else, let alone another country.

"Well, it's like this. Their father didn't like to work. So he packed up his eleven kids and moved the family to Mexico. You don't need much money to live there. They had nine more kids. He didn't work, but his kids did. The neighbors felt sorry for the family and gave them corn and vegetables during growing season. I've heard the older boys even hunted alligators."

"Oh my." I didn't know what to think. Would they speak English? Did they work? What kind of neighbors would they be? So again, change was happening just when I thought we were settled in.

I didn't have to wonder long. They moved in on Sunday. Well, at least they came to that house and slept on the floor. They didn't have much except bedrolls, dirty pillows, a banjo, and two wooden boxes of clothes. No furniture, no stove, or pots and pans, no dishes, no towels. How could they live this way?

Tom immediately invited them to supper. "What? How could I possibly feed two extra men? Where would I get that much food?"

Tom laughed and said, "Oh, you know how to stretch a biscuit. It'll be just fine."

He was right. There was enough. I believed in the miracle of the loaves and fish right then. We all ate and were satisfied. I was even able to whip up a pudding for dessert. The men retreated to our living room while I got busy with the dishes. At least we'd found a used davenport so they didn't have to sit on the floor. We were living like royalty compared to Curtis and Charlie.

I worked quietly as I listened to their unbelievable stories of growing up so poor that their mama even rendered lard from the alligators so they could fry their corn tortillas. "Alligator was pretty good," Charlie said. "But it couldn't touch the great supper we had today."

Hmm. Maybe I was going to like these cousins. I smiled as I cleaned up.

Come Monday morning, they rode with Tom out to the mill to put in their application for work. That was a good sign. At least they were willing to look for work. They were put on the "extra board," which meant they would be called to work when someone was sick or they had extra work. That also meant they might be working any shift, day or night.

Charlie was a good guy. He was respectful, kind and gave us newlyweds space. Curtis, however, was thinking himself a ladies' man. I could tell by the way he looked at me, making sure I noticed what he was saying or doing, and even at times would touch my arm when Tom wasn't around. He'd sit on their front porch and sing songs loudly to make sure I was listening. I hated the days when Tom was at work and Curtis was not. I'd go to the store or to town those days, avoiding rather than dealing with him. Why are men like that?

I received a letter from Papa on November 15. It said, "Susie, I hate to ask this, but could you come home and help us? Mama is very sick and hasn't been out of bed for three days. We need you to help." My heart pounded; I began to get a headache. All I could think of was, I've got to go help my mama. I rushed into the bedroom and grabbed the old suitcase and began throwing clothes in. I heard a knock on the front door. Who was that? Too early for Tom to be home. He wouldn't knock.

"Susie, you here?" A familiar voice called. My brother! I hadn't seen Johnny since I got married. He was always working on some get-rich scheme. Right now he was selling newspapers. I came out of the bedroom with the suitcase in my hands. I looked at his face and knew Papa had sent him to get me.

"I had to come to Lewiston to pick up papers," he said casually. "Papa asked if I . . . if I could . . . could bring you back home. Mama's not doing well. Papa's afraid . . ." He hung his head. "Can you come?"

"Of course, of course I'll come," I said without hesitation. "But I need to wait until Tom gets home. I can't just run off and leave him. Sit and I'll get some dinner started. He'll be home soon." I bustled into the kitchen, stoked the stove, and started peeling potatoes. "Tell me about Mama," I called to Johnny.

He ambled out to the kitchen and sat at the table. "She's runnin' a fever. Can't keep anything down. Got the runs. Lost weight. She just stares at the ceiling. Can't talk above a whisper. We've been taking turns staying up at night with her. We're dog-tired. The house is a mess. We sent Edna to Grace and Jim's. Hate to admit it; we really miss you."

"I'll come. Tom will understand." I buzzed around the kitchen, thankful that I had baked that day and food-shopped yesterday. That was hard to get used to since I had always lived where we had our own food. Tom would be okay. After all he had been a bachelor for five years before we got married. He would survive.

Johnny was finishing a big bowl of potato soup and a slice of bread when Tom pulled in. The first thing he saw was the suitcase sitting in the middle of the living room. "What!" he cried out. I ran to hug him and quickly spilled the story of Papa's letter. "He sent Johnny to get me. My mama needs me." I pleaded with my eyes.

Johnny stepped from the kitchen and shook Tom's hand. "She's so sick. . .," and he began to cry. It was overwhelming to see my brother crying tears of concern over someone else, not his fake crocodile tears of feeling sorry for himself.

Tom read the letter, and wrapped me in his big strong arms. "You go help your family. I'll miss you so much." We stood in silence that way until I remembered the food.

"There's potato soup on the back of the stove, I baked today, I went to the store . . ."

"Here, I'll help carry your suitcase out." Tom wrapped his arm around my waist, and we walked to Johnny's car. "I'll miss you. Oh, man, will I miss you, Susie. Write every day. I hope your mama gets well quick." With tears spilling down our cheeks, we kissed goodbye. I climbed in the car and waved until he could no longer be seen. The ride was quiet. I couldn't talk. Married only a month and having to leave my husband was the saddest thing I'd ever done.

I thought when we were almost to the homestead, at least I won't have to worry about avoiding Curtis. Maybe he'll find a job someplace else and move before I get back.

Chapter 26

Influenza

November winters in the high country were much different from the valley. I stepped from the car and plunged into snow up to my knees. "Brrrr!" I scolded myself for forgetting so quickly. I hadn't even brought my boots.

I waded to the house. Papa met me at the door and hugged me until I thought he would never let go. "She's so sick, Susie. I can't lose her. Got to pray and keep trusting God." He broke into prayer as we walked. My papa, my prayer partner who had prayed me through many hard times, was now asking God to save my mama. I knew God heard.

He led me into the parlor where they'd made a bed for her when she got too weak to climb the stairs. In the dim light she could have been a corpse, eyes open, staring, skin white as the muslin sheets she was lying on. I knelt beside her and took her cold hand. "Mama, I'm here. I've come home to take care of you." There was no response. I touched her head. It was burning. How could her hands be so cold and her head so hot? I wasn't a doctor. I was only eighteen. What should I do? My mind flew back to those days of my yellow jaundice. The doctor told Mama to put cold wet clothes on my face. Snow. There's cold snow. We could pack a sock with snow and put it on Mama's forehead.

I told Papa to go get some sleep and promised I'd wake him if there was a change. Reluctantly he shuffled upstairs. I found some wool gloves and laid them on the wood stove. When they were warm, I slipped them on her hands. I felt her feet. Ice cold! I covered her feet with warm socks.

I found an old sock in the mending drawer and with a big spoon, filled it from the snow piled up against the porch. How odd to be putting hot on one part of the body and cold on the other. I put another blanket on her then prayed and waited. I replaced the snow every few minutes when it started to melt; rewarming the mitts and socks every time I got snow. All winter nights are long, but this was the longest, darkest night of my life.

It was just light enough that I could see the barn when I heard footsteps coming down the stairs—Papa. I looked at Mama. Her eyes were closed, and she seemed to be breathing easier. I hadn't put the sock on her head since dawn first started to break. I reached over and touched her head. It was warm but not burning. The fever still hadn't broken. I gave Papa a hug as he went to sit by her bed. I wrung out the wet sock, filled it, and brought it back. Papa took it from me and gently placed it on Mama. Feeling the cold, she stirred. Her eyes sprung open, she turned her head toward him and croaked, "Cold." Papa stroked her hair and sang to her while keeping the sock in place.

Keeping the same routine going broke the fever around suppertime. Sweat drenched her gown and bedding. Papa helped me give her a warm sponge bath and held her while I changed the bedding. Tears poured down our cheeks, and we sang praises to God. We knew the worst was over.

Johnny went to his room when we arrived the night before. Papa and I ate hard biscuits and sausage gravy. I started some chicken broth from the larder. Mama needed to eat. Everyone knows chicken soup's the best thing when you're sick. I fed her with an eyedropper, one drop at a time, around a tablespoon the first time, every hour a little more. Finally she shook her head, closed her eyes, and went into a deep restful sleep.

Influenza—that's what the doctor called it. Many people on the prairie had come down with it. That's why he hadn't been able to get to our house sooner. Seven had died so far. It wasn't as bad as ten years ago when we lost thirty-two in our community, mostly elderly and babies. He was relieved to see Mama awake, taking water and broth, and talking. "You did good. It will be a while 'til she can be out of bed. She's weak. Don't let her walk alone. Only liquids at first then soft food." He gave us some liquid medicine and more instructions. "You are very lucky, Minnie," he told Mama.

"It wasn't luck," Papa said. "It was the good Lord and Susie."

Doc smiled and nodded. "She's out of the woods. Call me if there's a change." He packed his bag, mounted his horse, and left for the next farm. The dreaded illness hadn't left any family untouched. School and church meetings, dances, and literaries had all been canceled. We were isolated in hopes of stopping its spread.

Tom! In taking care of Mama, I had forgotten to write to Tom. I knew he would be pacing the floor and stewing. Even though I had been up over thirty hours, I quickly wrote a note to my husband:

> My dear sweety-pie,
> I got to the place safe and sound. Mama wasn't good at all.
> I packed snow on her face and heated gloves and socks for
> her hands and feet. She was so bad, she didn't even know
> I was there. Her fever finally broke this evening. The doc
> came and said she's over the worst. I miss you so much.
> I love you so much. I'll write more tomorrow after I get
> some sleep.
> Your loving wife, Susie

Sleep came quickly. When I woke up, I smelled bacon and coffee. It took me a minute to remember where I was. I quickly dressed and went downstairs. Papa had fixed breakfast. Mama sat in bed with pillows propping her up. She was finishing a small bowl of soupy Cream of Wheat. I took it from her shaky hands. "Let me get that, Mama. Looks like you ate good." She fixed her blue eyes on me and smiled weakly. "Yes," she croaked. Then she closed her eyes and nodded off.

There was much to do around the house. I cleaned, scrubbed, washed clothes, and cooked. Edna came home the third day after I arrived. I was excited to see my little girl. Goodness how she had grown in just four weeks.

We talked and talked while I worked. Looking back, it seemed strange Edna didn't help. She certainly was capable at age ten. After all, when I was ten I was in charge of taking care of her, as a two-year-old, plus keeping the house clean. I guess we still thought of her as being the baby of the family. Babies don't need to work when adults are around.

A week without my dear sweetie pie was all I could stand. I had to go home. Home? I suddenly realized that in just five weeks, my mind had shifted "home" from Mama and Papa to my place with Tom. I kissed Mama's forehead and told her goodbye. I promised to come back in three days. For the first time in my life, she looked into my eyes and said, "Thank you, Susie." My mama had thanked me! My heart choked with tears as I rode the train to Lewiston.

Chapter 27

Another Change

In the next month I traveled more than I had in my entire life. Three days in Clarkston, four days at the folks. The winter allowed Mama to take over housekeeping bit by bit. I tried to do extra baking, deep cleaning, and such when I was there.

The second week of December when Tom picked me up at the train station, he drove to a different house. He'd moved us while I was gone. I no longer had to pray Curtis and Charlie would move. This small house on Second Street was next to another of Tom's cousins, Orville Roe. He was married to a tiny lady named Ada who just happened to have a sister who was married to Tom's brother, Stanley. It gets very complicated when you're from a small town. Ada and I quickly became good friends. She reminded me of my school friend, Avis; small, strong-willed, independent, and fun. We could talk for hours.

One night when Orville and Tom were working the graveyard shift at the mill, Ada and I decided to stay overnight at her house. After crawling in bed, we talked for hours before falling asleep. Unfortunately, Orville got off early. He didn't want to wake his wife so didn't turn on a light. Can you imagine my shock when I felt the covers lift and this big man started to crawl in bed beside me? I screamed, "Oh, no! Ada, Ada . . ."

"What's going on?" shouted Orville who was usually soft-spoken.

Ada began to laugh. I joined her, laughing so hard we couldn't get out of bed. Poor Orville was embarrassed and confused, plus exhausted from a hard night at work.

Finally Ada caught her breath enough to order, "Honey, go in the living room so Susie can get dressed." I quickly made my escape and crawled into my own bed next door, still laughing. We never let Orville forget the night that he tried to get in bed with two women.

Christmas in 1928 became a difficult discussion. "I want to
go home for Christmas," I insisted.

"Why?" countered Tom. "You're already there more than here."

"I know. I'm sorry, but it will get better. I need to be with my family; it's Christmas," I argued.

Christmas at the Kole household meant extended family, feasting for at least three days, visiting all of my cousins, singing, dancing. It wouldn't be Christmas any place else.

"Okay," Tom finally conceded. "We'll celebrate Christmas with your family and go to my family's for New Year's." That decision set the pattern for the rest of our lives.

We rode the train. Papa picked us up. I'd saved enough money from groceries to buy gifts. How great to live in the big city and buy things not available in the small town of Reubens. I was proud to buy our first gifts as a couple. Tom was proud to prove to my family that he could not only take care of me, but also provide gifts for everyone. We thought we were doing well.

At the end of January 1929, the mill began laying off workers, meaning no work for Tom. What would we do? Tom only knew farming and mill work. His father pulled him out of school at the end of third grade to work on their farm. Thank goodness his mother and father had sold their farm and moved to a house on the river just above the Lewiston mill. I shuddered just thinking about possibly living in the same house as my father-in-law.

Tom came home one day and announced, "Susie, we're movin' to the Lame place." In those days, farms were called by the last name of the original owner, no other address. The Lame and Kole families had been close friends for a long time. I'd visited their farm many times. There was a large house and around sixty acres.

"How can we farm? We don't have horses, equipment, or seed," I questioned.

"Don't worry. I have family," was his reply.

"Yes, and I have Jesus," I affirmed.

There was an immediate dark cloud on Tom's face. "Ya don't think I can take care of us?"

"I'm . . . I'm sorry. I just meant that He'll help us."

"Don't need no help," grumbled Tom.

It was a silent week as we packed our belongings in the wooden boxes and prepared to move. I was learning there were subjects I couldn't mention—God, his father, his ability to do something, and questions about the future. Tom threw up "the silent wall" any time he felt I was criticizing or thought him incapable. It would take at least a week to tear it down. I'd pray, "Jesus, help me be loving and kind." It would be another lonely time, a time when I learned to chatter on to myself, not expecting a response. I became a polished actress, sticking to my scripted lines, plastering on a smile, and keeping busy.

Life never seems to be without challenge. Now that I'd built a bridge of love and acceptance with my mama, I found myself in another dilemma: my husband's silent wall. His Chase stubbornness constantly had me walking on eggshells. As I learned more about their family, I began to understand "the wall" was survival. In my time around his brothers and sisters, I realized, I wasn't alone in this struggle. It ran like an epidemic in the Chase family. Anyone married into it received "the wall" treatment from time to time. Their house wasn't an easy place to grow up. The silence hid secrets of abuse: emotional, physical, mental, and sexual. All the while they went to the little church in the closest town, singing hymns, and putting on the "good family" face. Some turned to God when they left home. Others turned away. The silent retreat became a safe place to hide for each of the Chase children regardless of their relationship with God.

Chapter 28

The Market Came Tumbling Down

October 24, 1929, the stock market crashed. That seemed a million miles away, too far to affect us. We heard on the radio about people jumping out windows, diving off bridges, committing suicide. Seemed unreal to us. These people must have worshiped their money, expecting it to save them.

Being poor was a blessing. We'd been poor most of our lives. Every penny was important. We relied on the resources God gave us to supply our needs. We were farmers who knew how to grow, how to save, how to do without. "How to get by in a pinch," as Mama would say.

The Lame place was not successful. It gave us shelter, a garden, a horse, cow, chickens, and a way to earn some money by selling milk, eggs, and vegetables. Mr. and Mrs. Lame, in their eighties, had moved to Lewiston to live with their daughter. We were the caretakers until the family decided what to do with the farm. They didn't want us to plant and harvest.

In May of 1930, the oldest boy decided he would take over. We were again without a home or a livelihood.

"Do you have a plan, Tom?" I carefully worded my question.

"Heard 'bout a new government program in town last week. I wanna find out more. I'm gonna go to town." He climbed on Blacky. "Be back tomorrow evening. Keep the soup hot."

I had learned in our year and half of marriage that Tom was fiercely independent and proud, to the point of being the most stubborn person

I'd ever met. Since he was the middle child of seven, Tom's father saw no use for him to go to school because he was slow. He was pulled out of school after the third grade to work on the Chase farm. When he didn't work hard enough or fast enough, his father beat him.

One day his mother was coming from the garden with an apron full of corn. She heard yelling and crying in the barn. Stepping to the doorway, she saw Albert beating Tom with a chain. She grabbed an ear of corn, took aim, and hit her husband square in the temple, knocking him out. Without a word, she led Tom to the house, cleaned him up, and put ointment on his back. It surprised no one that Tom began at the early age of twelve to work for other farmers in the area more than for his father. He earned his own way, dependent on no one. His hard work and reliability made him in demand as a farmhand.

I knew Tom would do his best to take care of me. One month to find a home and a job? I trusted my husband, but not like I trusted my Jesus. I spent the night talking to Him. "Jesus, we're needing a lot of help right now. We don't ask much. We need shelter and food. That's all I'm asking for."

The next day dragged. Rain forced me inside most of the time. I fed the Lames' animals, built a fire, and set to putting our few belongings into the wooden boxes given us as a wedding present.

The setting sun was leaving long shadows across the yard when I spied Tom coming up the dirt road on Blacky. He rode bent over, soaked to the skin, cold, tired, and hungry. It's too bad we didn't have gas for the car. His feeble smile wasn't reassuring. He led Blacky to the barn. I rushed inside to dip up supper.

"Here's the deal," he began as he slurped down the watery soup. "The government's lookin' fer people to cut down and clear Indian land. We can live on the land for five years if we cut down fifteen acres of lodgepole pine. We can do whatever we want with the trees, but in the end it's got to be ready to plant crops on."

I was speechless. Is this the answer to my prayer? Seemed a bit harsh. No shelter, no food, just fifteen acres covered with trees.

"How are we going to do that?" I asked. "How do you cut down trees?" The area where I'd grown up was prairie. The trees we had, we cherished. They were fruit trees the folks planted when they first married. I began to giggle.

"What're ya laughin' at?"

"I was just thinking about George Washington. I can see Thomas Albert Chase out there with his mighty hatchet, chopping down trees."

Tom smiled. "Well, nice to be compared to our first president instead of Paul Bunyan. Might be able to live up 'ta that picture. George was just a kid."

Then he became serious. "I'm gonna trade the car for some tools. We're needin' a pick, shovel, axe, hatchet, chisel, measuring stick, and a crosscut saw. Oh, and a stove."

I took a deep breath, swallowed hard, and responded, "You know what's best, Tom. I'm your wife. I trust you."

"Not sure I like those words. Not sure I can live up to the responsibility. Not sure at all." Tom shook his mop of black hair.

"Hey, kiddo. We can do it. We can do anything." I tried my best to cheer him up, but inside I was saying, *Oh, God. What have we gotten ourselves into?*

Chapter 29

The Stick Ranch

We moved to our fifteen acres, which we affectionately called "the Stick Ranch" on June 3. It sat on the hill halfway between Culdesac and Reubens, east of the dirt road. A smelly, brown canvas tent, borrowed from Tom's brother, Stanley, became our home. A twenty-four-inch round potbelly stove sat in the middle with a stove pipe reaching up through the carefully planned hole in the center to keep the tent from catching fire. It had two purposes—cooking and warmth. Tom built a tent frame from small trees while I was visiting the folks. He framed a bed, stuffed a tic full of dry grass for a mattress, and built a small table and sat our oil lamp in the middle of it. No chairs yet. Our wooden packing boxes became shelves stacked against the other side of the tent. There was barely enough room to turn around. I would not complain. It was a place to live, and we could improve it. After all, we'd be staying here five years.

At the ages of almost twenty and twenty-five, we tackled our first project, a log cabin. The goal was to have it built before winter set in. "Eat up," I commanded as I handed Tom a large bowl of oatmeal. "We need all the energy we can get."

Dishes were quickly done, and we marched off to begin our house. Neither of us had building experience, but I could tell Tom had been thinking a lot. "Now look at that tree right over there," he pointed to the closest tree. "See, it's 'bout two feet across. The way I figure, it'll take six logs, two for the foundation and four high on each wall. What da ya think?"

I gulped and my heart flip-flopped as my eyes followed the tree to the top. "Tall, really tall," was all I could reply.

"Yep, round seventy feet they tell me. There's scads of trees. We can make a big house." I glanced at his face shining with anticipation and realized this was a great adventure for him. To me, it was more like a nightmare.

Tom had asked around Culdesac how to go about this. The old men sitting in front of the general store were happy to share all their building knowledge, even if they'd never built anything bigger than a chicken coup.

"We got 'ta dig ditches for the foundation." He handed me the shovel and took up the pick and a big ball of string. "Gonna mark it with string where to dig." He began to unravel the string in the clearing next to the dirt road.

"How are you going to know the lines are straight or if they'll come together at the right place?" I was doubtful already.

Tom whistled as he measured a long piece of string, cut it, and used it to cut five more. I sat on a grassy spot and watched. The sounds of bees, birds, and wind in the treetops blended with Tom's tune, filling my heart with peace. Yes, we can do this.

So with pick and shovel, we dug. It was slow going. The ground was hard and rocky. Tom loosened the rocks with the pick. I stacked them beside the ditch; Tom scooped out the dirt. By noon we had finished around four feet of the first trench.

"I'd better get some dinner." I looked at my filthy hands. We'd brought two cream cans of water with us. I hated to wash with it, but I must. I stoked the fire and put some water on to boil for soup. I must be careful with supplies. There were some canned vegetables left from the Lame place, but who knew how long it would be before there was any more. It was too late to prepare land for planting.

My hands ached from rock picking. I could hear Tom brushing off his clothes and hands outside the open flap. He ducked in, smiled weakly, and gave me a hug. "This ain't gonna to be easy. Who knew rocks was part of the deal." We both laughed. We had no idea how hard it was going to get.

By the end of June, the ditches were dug. Tom borrowed a level from the Zhalbers, our nearest neighbor, to make sure they were the same depth all the way around. July 3, we cut down our first tree. Tom cut a notch on the side of the tree in the direction we wanted it to fall.

"Okay, Susie. Grab the handle on that end, one hand above the other. When you push, push the blade into the tree." I'd never used a crosscut saw before. It was six feet long with large handles on each end. Definitely a two-man saw, or in this case, a man and woman saw. It looked daunting. Back and forth, back and forth, back and forth. Our rhythm was awkward and jerky, complicated by the fact Tom was left handed and I was right. Aching arms, legs, and backs. At the end of the day the first lodgepole pine came crashing down. We whooped and hollered at our success, gave each other a hug and kiss, then looked at our first conquest.

There was a huge problem; about halfway up, the tree tapered. The second half was much smaller around than the first half. "Well," Tom shrugged. "Got two choices. If we wanna build it as big as the ditches, we have ta cut twice as many trees or we can dig more ditches across and make a smaller cabin. What do ya think?"

I was so tired of picking and piling rocks. "Cut more trees!"

"I was hope'n ya'd say that."

The next morning we measured our tree, cut it, stripped the bark, and painted it with hot tar to help preserve the wood underground. We hitched Blacky to the thirty-five-foot log and moved it into the first ditch. Tom chiseled out a notch to fit the next log into. We packed the rocks back around the edges to make it stable. We were on our way. We only finished one tree every two days. The top half, we cut into eight-foot lengths and make fence posts to build a pen for Blacky.

Tom built a pole-sled, piled ten fence posts on it, hooked up Blacky, and hauled them to Culdesac to sell for two pennies apiece. "Don't forget the water," I'd call as Tom mounted Blacky for the hour's trip to town. Ten poles was Blacky's limit for pulling, so a round trip would gain twenty cents and cost two hours of time. Tom stopped at the spring just off the dirt road to get fresh water in the milk cans.

What would we do without our faithful horse who'd been given to us by the Lames for taking care of their place? By day, we tied him to a tree where he could eat grass. By night, he went in the pen with a little shelter on one end. How would we feed him in the winter? I began to worry about how I would feed us.

We did take out time to go to the Winchester's Fourth of July picnic. Even though most of the young people had grown up and left the area, they came back for the Fourth celebration every year—except last year. Edna had come down with chickenpox, and Johnny had caught smallpox while working at the Stephens' place. He was mighty sick. Mrs. Stephens was nursing him and her husband back from the brink of death after three weeks of high fevers. Both of these diseases were making the rounds on the Camas Prairie. Fear dominated events. No big celebration for America in 1929.

There was a horrible tragedy came out of that smallpox round. Mr. Lowe and Mr. Virgil had been having a heated argument over water rights on their farms. Each thought the other's well was drawing too much water, and they weren't getting their fair share. It got so bad between them, everyone thought they were going to have an outright duel. It turned worse than that. Mr. Lowe's wife came down with smallpox. She nearly died but survived with huge scabs all over her body. Mr. Lowe took some of those scabs and mailed them to Mr. Virgil in an envelope, hoping he would get the pox. It would serve him right for being so stubborn. Mr. Virgil's curious three-year-old daughter opened the envelope and played with the strange things she found inside. Can you imagine her mother's horror when she discovered what her little girl had in her hands? Yes, she contracted smallpox. Yes, she died. It brought unbelievable grief to the community. Mr. Lowe had such remorse over what had resulted from his anger, he committed suicide. Mr. and Mrs. Virgil left the area and never farmed again. It left a dark cloud over the whole area.

It was time to move on after the whole, sad affair. There had to be a great celebration in the year 1930 in spite of the Depression.

Chapter 30

Friends, Old and New

Visitors stopped by now and then to check on our progress and give us pointers. Two regulars from Culdesac were Delmar and Charlie when they made deliveries to the general store in Reubens. They sometimes brought us flour, coffee, or a bit of salt or sugar, which we paid for with our precious "two-pence-a-pole" money. With the Depression still going on, a bag of flour was twenty-five cents, sugar, ten cents. We counted the cost in labor and poles. Our one luxury was coffee, twenty-cents a can. Tom had to have his coffee each morning. I never developed the taste. We used the grounds over and over until it no longer tasted like coffee. Generally one-fourth cup of boiled grounds lasted a week depending on how many visitors we had. It was always the polite thing to offer a cup of coffee.

Early on we discovered the property we were clearing was on a hunting trail. Members of the Nez Perce tribe often followed it to their favorite hunting ground. My first Indian visitor gave me quite a start one day when Tom was in town. I was packing rocks into the trench when I had the odd feeling I was being watched. I stood and spotted a very large native watching me. How could he and his horse creep up so silently on me? I froze in fear. Then I remembered Grandma's wise, simple advice, "If you are kind and treat people nice, they will be nice to you."

"Hello," I said. "Would you like a cup of coffee?" I had no idea if he even knew what coffee was or if he understood me. We stood there eyeing each other for a long time. Finally he grunted. I took that as a yes, walked confidently into the tent, poured a shaky cup of coffee, and brought it out, extending it toward him. I thought he'd never respond. He nodded, then warily walked over and took the cup. Never a word was spoken as he sat on a log outside our tent and drank. It was the first of his unannounced visits to our tent home. Eventually he brought friends to share our hospitality.

As we sat on our tree-stump stools by our table one late August morning, I watched Tom pour the coffee from his cup into his saucer and loudly slurp it. *Is this really going to work*, I thought. *God, I'm so tired, I hurt so bad, I'm hungry. I miss my family and friends. I'm not sure how much longer I can do this.*

God in His usual reassuring way answered, *I am with you.*

Tom and I, with Blacky's help, managed to stack one row of logs on top of the foundation by the end of August. Our pride couldn't show through the disappointment of slow progress. We had only the possibility of one more good month before snow in these mountains. We would never make it by ourselves, let alone the impossible task of getting the logs on the higher rows.

It was a Sunday morning. We always allowed ourselves to sleep in until seven o'clock on Sunday. When I woke up, Tom was up and gone. He left a note: Gone to town to see if we can get some help. I knew that hurt his pride something fierce.

I began to chink between the logs. At least that was something I could do by myself. The other thing I could do was talk to God. "God, this seems impossible. Can't see us getting this done before winter. I've just got to believe all things are possible. That's what you said. I've just got to trust you. Sorry for not understanding how you're going to work this out. Help me not to complain. Help me not to make Tom feel bad. This is what we've got and it's better than nothing so I thank you for it . . ."

I chinked, cried, and talked the whole day. I never let Tom see me cry. It would upset him. Besides, I had my pride too. If he could do this, so could I.

At almost nightfall, I heard Blacky plodding up to the lodgepole pen. Tom talked to him as he curried him down and put water and food out for him. Sometimes he would stop on the way home and pick apples from the wild trees along the road. He always shared with Blacky. The ones he'd been bringing were green. Maybe they were getting ripe. I stepped outside, anticipating good news. After all I'd been praying all day. God was going to take care of us. Right?

Tom glanced over at me but didn't say a word. I couldn't read the expression on his face. Was it a yes or a no? Help or not? He put away the curry comb, shut the gate, and waded through the tall grass. This was strange behavior, even for Tom. I couldn't stand it any longer, "Well?" I finally asked.

Tom sighed, looked me in the eyes, then broke out in a big grin. "We've got men!" he shouted.

"What?" I couldn't believe it. "When? How many? How long?" questions poured out of my mouth.

"Got anything to eat? I'm starved." Tom headed into the tent.

I ran after him. "Of course, of course. I'm sorry. I should have thought . . ." I quickly sliced up some flat bread that I made that morning and poured him a thick, black cup of coffee that sat on the stove since Friday.

"Now, please tell me?" I sat down on the other stump. "Ouch," I winced. Stumps aren't easy sitting when you've been chinking all day.

"All right," Tom started after he stuffed another piece of bread in. "Charlie says he can get twelve to fourteen men up here to have a wall-raisin' party in about two weeks when harvest is over. They can only spare a day, but he thinks they can set all the logs if they work from sunup to sundown."

"Oh, my. Twelve to fourteen men. How are we going to feed them? I only have a half bag of dried beans left from what Mrs. Zhalber gave us last month." As I was a woman, my mind naturally went to food and feeding men.

"Delmar said, 'Don't fuss about food. The men'll bring their own.' We're lucky to have good friends willin' to help. There's one catch." Oh, oh, I thought. "We have 'ta pay each man a dollar for the day."

I was speechless. Panic set in. Of course we'd need to pay them. How could we expect them to do backbreaking labor without any pay? "But Tom, we've only been able to save nineteen dollars from our fence posts.

That only leaves us with . . ." I couldn't finish. How could we survive the winter with five dollars and no food, even if the house was finished?

"There's something else," Tom took my small, rough hand, "We have to have the logs cut, peeled, and notched so they can lift 'em into place." Oh my, oh my! I kept thinking. Fourteen days to get sixteen logs ready. "We'll do it like this," he continued. "We'll down the trees, cut the bottom half into thirty-five-foot logs, peel 'em where they fall, then have Blacky pull 'em to the cabin area. We'll leave the top half there and not worry 'bout 'em till later. We can do it. The bottom part doesn't have a whole lot of limbs to cut off. We won't be makin' poles 'till the logs are finished. We can do it, Susie."

His enthusiasm was catching. "Yes, of course we can!"

The days blurred—back and forth, back and forth, peel, peel, peel, notch, notch, notch, move into place. Each night we counted notches we carved on the log outside our tent, keeping track of days. Exhaustion took over mind and body. There wasn't a single spot that didn't hurt as I fell into bed every night.

Together we counted the logs. "What! Sixteen!" We counted again. "What day is it?" I counted the bench notches, "Day twelve. Whoopi!"

We slept in the next morning. When we woke, we found a pheasant lying on our outside log bench. It had been shot with an arrow.

Chapter 31

The Wall Raising

The trees were downed, cut, peeled, notched, and moved into place by the fourteenth day. Tom took our two cream cans and every other available pot to fill with water at the spring. I boiled the pheasant gift and cooked the beans with it for dinner.

We were up before dawn. Neither of us slept well, anticipating the day. At daylight, the first car chugged up the road. Out piled four big, coveralled men dragging ropes and rigging. A Model T putted up with two men in front and four seated in the back on tool boxes they brought, just in case. Bringing up the rear was a coupe with two in front and a third stuffed in the rumble seat. Thirteen plus Tom. The army of workers swarmed over to the cabin site like bees to a lone flower.

George took on the role of crew boss. He walked around the two-log high walls, looked at us, and smiled. "Not bad for greenhorns, Tom. We'll get these on up in no time." I felt my husband stand a little taller and knew without looking that he was smiling. George assigned jobs. There was little for me to do but watch.

No need for Blacky to help either. He whinnied as the men rigged up pulleys, ropes, and levers. Fascinated, I tried to understand, but finally gave up and went to stir the beans. Blacky's whinnies sounded more frantic as the men's voices shouted directions. What in the world was going on? I stepped from the tent just in time to see our horse hit the pole fence at a dead run, break through, and disappear into the forest.

"Blacky!" yelled Tom, whistling for him to come.

"I'll find him! He's spooked by all the noise. You just keep working." I tore into the woods following the crashing of trampled underbrush. The sound led me downhill and the racket of men working became dim and faded. Then, there was only silence. Good, I thought. He's stopped. "Blacky," I spoke quietly. "Blacky, it's me. It's going to be all right. I'm right here. There's nothing to be afraid of." I treaded lightly on down the hill then stopped. What if he went another direction? Turning round and around, I strained my ears for clues. I sat on a log and listened. Nothing. I picked a few late-season huckleberries and popped them in my thirsty mouth. A breaking branch crackled behind me. Quickly turning, I was startled by a black bear also enjoying berries. Freeze, Susan, I told myself. I'd always been told to freeze. Mr. Bear seemed oblivious to me as he stuffed his mouth. Breathing was impossible. How long? What next? He kept eating, moving away from me to another patch of delightful treats. Time forever stood still.

Horse hooves coming up the hill jerked me out of my trance. The bear was forgotten as I quietly picked my way toward the sound and came to a trail. A trail? This must be the hunting trail. I breathed deep. Out from the trees came my Indian friend mounted on his Appaloosa, leading our runaway. I let out a squeal. "Boy, am I glad to see you. You've found Blacky! Thank you, thank you. There was this bear . . ." I rambled on and on releasing all my bear-tension into words. When I had exhausted my vocabulary, I ended with, "Thank you, friend." From that day on that's what we called him—Friend.

Friend nodded, grunted, and helped me up on Blacky. We rode silently to the clearing. Work came to a halt as we rode out of the trees and across the cut area. Tom rushed over, lifted me down, and thanked my rescuer. "Friend," I smiled at Tom. "His name is going to be Friend." Friend grunted again, nodded, and rode on.

"Just make sure that's all he is." Tom muttered as he turned back to work.

After tying Blacky to a tree, I checked out the progress. Goodness, had I been gone that long? Two walls were finished. I hurried in to check on the beans. The fire was low. That was good. Kept them from burning.

Another car arrived as I stepped out of the tent. More men? No, it was three of the wives. The driver was my cousin, Katherine. I greeted her with a warm hug. "I didn't know you could drive!"

"It took a lot of persuading to get Delmar to teach me," she laughed. "He still won't ride with me." They began unloading food onto the log bench in front of the tent.

What a wonderful surprise! This was just like thrashing bees on the farm. I brought out my pot of beans. "I've only got two plates," I confessed. "What are they going to put their food on?"

"Never mind," Maggie winked. "It's all taken care of."

George called, "Dinner!" Work stopped and the men traipsed to the cars, retrieving their own tin plates with a fork and spoon. Smart idea, I thought. We're having the best picnic ever.

The finest part was visiting. I hadn't been around friends to visit for over a year. I was hungry for women talk. I amazed them with my bear adventure. They told about their comfortable, settled lives in the city of Culdesac. It was a good afternoon.

Four walls, eight feet high, stood strong and steady when the workers left that afternoon. Tom gave each a dollar for his hard work. The men climbed into the cars and headed back to the security of their comfortable homes. We retreated into our smelly, brown tent.

Chapter 32

A Family Addition

The silent treatment moved into our tent. I expected this after his comment about Friend. Our days fell back to normal routine; Tom making poles from trees lying on the ground and my mixing sawdust with clay and water, chinking, chinking, chinking. No words passed between us. On the third day, ten poles were loaded to take to town. I had to say goodbye. I strode over as he was preparing to mount and kissed him on the cheek, "Have a good trip. Don't forget the water." There was no reaction. I turned back to the walls. Tears made muddy rivers down my cheeks as he rode away.

There was no comfort in being alone. Anger that I thought I had left in childhood swelled

Inside, and I filled the air with shouted complaints. "I never asked for this! None of my friends are living in a smelly, dirty tent and cutting down trees! Life's not s'posed to be like this! I need a home! I need children! I need a husband who talks to me! I wish I'd never gotten married! I can't do this! I can't do four and a half more years of this!" I screamed and cried myself into exhaustion, falling asleep on the lumpy grass tic in the tent, and awakening to the sound of horse's hooves.

The fire had gone out, the coffee was cold, there was no supper. Fear gripped my mind. I stoked the fire, hoping the coals were hot enough to ignite the kindling. I had to use a precious match to relight it. I began slicing four-day-old bread left by our workers. The hard bread was going to be a challenge to chew. A new, but familiar, sound pulled me out of the tent. Tom was currying down Blacky in the repaired pen and beside him stood a milk cow.

"What's this?" I ran full speed.

Tom grinned. "Has it been that long since you saw a cow?"

"What's it doing here? Is it lost? The owner must be worried . . ."

"Whoa, slow down, Susie. Stop talking." Tom put his hand on my mouth. "She's our cow." Speechless, my eyes shifted from the cow to my husband. His sparkling hazel eyes showed his delight in my shock. "Let's go git supper and I'll tell you 'bout the surprise cow."

"Supper? Oh . . . I'm afraid we'll have to . . . to finish up the leftovers . . . cold. The . . . fire went out." I stumbled over my words.

"I've got an idea." Tom fetched our biggest pail and went to the pen; pail in one hand and a stump in the other, he sat and began milking Bessy. Bessy, that was her name. Not very original. Every farmer had at least one Bessy in their herd. I hurried in the tent and continued to hack away on the stale bread. We'd have bread and warm milk. What better supper could you ask for?

Tom broke his bread into the bowl and covered it with the warm milk then began to explain about Bessy. "Delmar invited me ta' coffee at their house. When I walked in, there sat all the families that helped us with the walls. Seems the work crew decided we're needin' more help than just walls. They took up a collection and got us a cow."

We were rich! We had a horse, a cow, four walls on our house, a tent, a stove, and friends that cared. We were rich!

We had walls, but no roof. That wouldn't work in winter. Logs had to be cut into boards to make a roof. The closest mill was about thirty miles away in Winchester. Three dollars a log? Impossible! It might as well have been a million. Tom worked faster making poles, going to town every two days, but time was not our friend.

On the first Saturday of October, we woke up knowing we'd lost the race. The tent sagged and there was a cold smell in the air. It had snowed. Fortunately, Tom had bought flour, sugar, and oatmeal for us and oats and a salt lick for the animals yesterday when he took the poles in. Winter had arrived.

Snow—just in time for our second anniversary. In two years we had moved five times, going from life in the big city with running water and a warm house to living on Indian land in a freezing tent, two miles from the nearest water. At least snow could be melted. For better or worse, I kept telling myself.

"Got to make a better shelter for the animals," Tom announced as he pulled on his long-johns and dug out his winter ear-flapped hat. "We need to dig out some of those pole trees and make a bigger lean-to."

I found my boots the folks had given me last Christmas and used some string to tie my dress around my legs to keep it from dragging in the snow. "Sure would be nice to wear pants like men." I complained out loud. I followed him with the coping saw. "Never thought I'd ever say that. Ladies don't wear pants."

By nightfall, we had the animal shelter expanded into a three-sided lean-to to keep them warm and dry. "It's not the prettiest thing," Tom commented. "But it'll work."

Bless that little potbellied stove. It tried hard to put out heat, but it was impossible to keep the tent warm as it got colder and colder. At times there were so many layers of clothes on my body, I couldn't reach my feet to put my boots on.

Routine changed. Tom got up first every morning and pushed up on the tent roof to dump the night's accumulated snow. He built up the fire then went out to feed the animals. I shivered my way from under the covers, dipped a pan in the snow outside the door, and put it on the stove to melt for oatmeal and coffee. After breakfast, we went on a grass hunt, digging under snow for grass to pull for our livestock.

Afternoons were filled with hunting downed trees and making poles. Sawing got the blood pumping. What a great feeling to be warm. If the sun was shining, some layers of clothing were shed.

The first ten poles taken to town after the snow were left at Delmar and Katherine's, unsold. It hadn't dawned on us no one would be making fences with the ground frozen. What were we thinking? No source of income. We had nine dollars to get us and the livestock through the winter.

Survival. We just needed to survive the winter.

Chapter 33

Christmas Surprise

Christmas was bleak. We couldn't ride Blacky to the folks' house two hours away because Bessy had to be milked twice a day. "You go." Tom encouraged. "I'll stay here and milk. I'll be all right."

"I won't do that," I stubbornly protested. "You're my husband and I'll stay with you." We both dug in our heels so it was a moot point to argue. Besides, we'd missed some counting days on the log and weren't sure what day Christmas actually was. We agreed to celebrate in two more sleeps—whatever day that happened to be.

I'd been stingy with the flour during the last month. Who knew when we'd get to town or if we'd have enough money to buy it. I made pancakes for our Christmas dinner. I skimmed off the cream from the milk and made butter and dug out the last jar of unsweetened huckleberry jam. What a fine pancake feast! We sang a couple of Christmas carols with Tom's beautiful tenor voice and my soprano blending harmoniously. My heart felt refreshed and light. I decided we need to sing together more often.

Tom reached under his side of our sagging bed and handed me one of his socks. "What's this? You only want one sock washed?" I laughed. I felt something, reached inside, and pulled out a beautifully carved circle of wood and a smooth stick. "Oh, Tom, it's beautiful." I took off my gloves, pulled my curly, black hair back, and fastened it securely with the wooden tie. "How's it look? My ears are so warm with my hair tight against my head. What a perfect gift!" I gave him a kiss and hug.

"My turn. Close your eyes." I reached behind the last wooden box shelf and pulled out my gift. I'd been working on it for a month. With Tom being in the tent more, it was hard to find time. I laid a bundle of red wool in his hands. "Open," I commanded.

He slowly unrolled and unrolled what I thought might be the world's longest scarf. I had unraveled my red sweater and kept knitting until it was used up. Taking it from his hands, I gently wrapped it round and round his strong neck and tucked the ends down the front of his shirt. "Susie, what did I ever do to deserve such a wonderful wife." He held me close. We were warm inside and out.

"Listen." I pushed away from him. "Can you hear that?"

"It's bells ringing. I really must be in love." He laughed.

"No, it's sleigh bells." I threw on my outer coat. Tom followed suit. As we raised the tent flap, we were greeted by two black horses pulling a sleigh—my family!

"Whoa," Papa ordered as they came up to the tent. Edna popped out first and ran to give me a bear hug. Papa helped Mama climb down then Johnny jumped out. "Sorry we couldn't get here on Christmas," Papa started . . .

"So it's not Christmas?" I asked as I wrapped my arms around the first man in my life.

"Nope, that was yesterday. We had dinner at Maw's so there wasn't time to get here and back."

Mama waded along the path we'd stomped down the day before and wrapped me in her arms. Tears streaming down both our faces didn't freeze in the bright sunshine. All was well. My mama loved me. "My manners are terrible. Come in, come in." It was a tight fit. Bodies warmed the stuffy tent as we talked miles a minute. Tom brought in the milking stool so we could all sit.

"Johnny, go get the things out of the sleigh." Papa winked. A few minutes later, our little table was piled high. "We heard you was running low so we brought some supplies." There was flour, lard, eggs, rolled oats, chicken, bacon, steaks, and a ham. We would eat like royalty. Then, he came back with a can that made Tom's eyes light up—coffee. We'd been out for a month. The biggest surprise of all was a pie my little sister had baked. "There's food for the horse and cow out there too."

"I'll help get it." Tom left with Johnny. "Don't eat anything till I get back."

The folks hadn't been to our Stick Ranch. Many of the men on the prairie had moved to town, leaving Papa and Johnny to work long hours. Harvest had been late too. We kept in touch by mail. We were on a direct route from our place to theirs. The mailman picked up letters from me, dropped them off at the folks, then went on to Reubens to stay the night at Aunt Phoebe's hotel. He would stop back by the folks the next day to pick up their letters to us. It probably helped that the mailman was a close friend of the family. Delivery was fast, convenient, and never cost a dime. Letters had become the sunshine of my day; they were my family connection.

Now the folks were here. We found ourselves all wanting to talk at once. We chattered and laughed so loud that we didn't hear the horses whinnying to each other until we were quietly stuffing pie in our faces. Then we laughed at the horse conversation outside.

Mama had made Tom and me glove warmers, and Papa had bought new work gloves to put them in. What precious gifts. She also knitted foot warmers and nightcaps to wear to bed. So practical. So appreciated.

Three hours later, they fed the horses, climbed in the sleigh, and were off. It would be dark by the time they reached home, but the horses knew the way. What hope they had left with us! Love and hope, the greatest gifts of all.

Chapter 34

Survival

The end of January saw a huge dip in temperature. The old thermometer given to us on the Lame place registered ten below zero. Branches easily broke off in our hands, frozen solid. The challenge was keeping the animals warm. We tied two blankets on their backs with rope and hung the woodpile tarp across the front of the lean-to to shut out the wind. The cow no longer gave milk. The horse shivered constantly and gave us hopeless looks with his big brown eyes. We spent hours tearing away ice-crusted snow with the pick to break off grass for them. Thank God for the grain the folks had brought at Christmas.

Temperatures slid to fifteen below by the end of February's second week. We stacked wood inside, hoping it would dry quicker. Wet wood smolders and wheezes forever before catching fire. The woodpile dwindled, forcing us to hunt for old snags not buried in six feet of snow. We were surrounded by trees, but newly cut green wood doesn't burn at all. Our tent home was never what you'd call warm. It was especially body-shaking at night. The grass in our tic mattress froze, crunching with every move. We clung to every bit of heat we could find, never changing clothes, just adding layers.

One night, Tom, needing more body heat, reached over to wrap an arm around me. My cold body permeated even through layers of cloth. He touched my hands and face; they were frigid. "No. No. No!" he screamed, jumping out of bed. "I've killed my wife! She froze! She's dead!" He shot out the tent flap and ran circles, yelling, "I'm sorry, God.

I'm so stupid to think we could do this. Susie! Susie! You're gone! It's all my fault. She's frozen. She's frozen. No! No!"

I woke with a start to the screaming. "Tom!" I yelled but he couldn't hear. "Tom!" Reluctantly, I crawled out of bed and looked out the flap, "Tom! What in the world is going on? Have you lost your mind?"

In the dawn light, I saw him stop and stare as if I were a ghost. He grabbed me and began to sob, "It's you, it's really you. I thought I'd lost you."

We lost reality in the next few weeks. Our Christmas gift food was gone except for a little flour. Snow, cold, hunger. It was getting easy to give in, quit the fight. In our survival stupor, we didn't notice the rising temperatures.

What now? I awoke to a strange sound on the tent. Rain! It was raining! "Tom, Tom, wake up! It's raining!" Water falling from the sky never looked so good. In two days, it washed away most of the earth's white blanket, letting green grass show its tiny head. Hope sprang up with the grass. We had survived. The problem of food still reared its ugly head. We led Blacky and Bessy out to the greenest spot we could find. They chowed down, picking the earth bare. We spent painstaking hours brushing their thick, matted winter coats.

Tom set squirrel traps. We hadn't seen any out of hibernation, but we wanted to be ready. Not my favorite food, but hunger changes preferences. I don't think I could stoop so low as eating mice. Well, maybe.

The top part of fallen trees not finished last fall were visible. Saw, chop, peel. Saw, chop, peel . . . one post finished, then needing a rest. Our weak bodies resisted work. We fell exhausted into bed each night. Winter took a toll on both of us. Shrunken bodies were revealed as layers of clothes came off in the warmth of the sun. I was swimming in my dresses. I weighed in at ninety-eight pounds on the grain scale when I made a trip to the folks' farm in April.

Friend hadn't been through the area since the first big snow last fall. He was smart enough to store up for winter. It reminded me of the story "The Ant and the Grasshopper." Guess who we were? As we finished up the last treetop, Friend rode up. He sat watching us, then slowly climbed down. With a grunt, he pointed to something in the clearing. He kneeled and began to dig with his knife. He pulled up a root, handed it to me, grunted and pointed to the bulb. "Can we eat this?" I made eating motions with my hand. He nodded and pointed to the pan I was using to gather the last of the snow. "Cook?" He nodded again, mounted and moved on down the hunting trail. We gathered more and boiled, what we later found out, were camas roots. Not too tasty but satisfying. Two days later, we found a hind quarter of a deer on our log bench. Our Indian friend continued to live up to his name.

Chapter 35

Johnny's News

A surprise visitor drove up in the middle of May—my brother. Mama had sent him to deliver some canned beans, peas, and carrots. Yum! Vegetables to go with the deer. It's almost a complete meal. All we needed were potatoes. Johnny handed me carefully marked envelopes of seeds—a gift as good as gold. I had great plans for those jewels. The frozen ground was still too hard to dig up, but I determined not to be a grasshopper another winter.

"Looks like you've been working hard." Johnny shuffled his feet, not looking me in the eye. "You sure picked a dad-burned time to be pioneers. Not me. I don't even want to be a farmer."

"Don't say that, Johnny. Papa's counting on you taking over the place," I scolded.

"Can't do it. Want to be a salesman. Fuller Brush. Papa's buying the inventory for me to get started."

"How can you possibly make a living selling brushes?" Unbelievable, I thought. He'd already tried selling McNess, newspapers, and who knows what else. He borrowed money from Papa to get supplies; got tired of pushing flavors, drinks, and papers; quit and never paid it back. That had been crop money needed for the next year. Now he's borrowing against this year's crop. Whatever Johnny wants, Johnny gets, no matter whom he hurts. I felt the old jealous anger begin to boil.

"I'm moving to Lewiston. Can't sell nothing out here in no man's land." He still wouldn't look at me. "There's something else I want to tell you . . ." I waited. "Alice and I are getting married."

"What? Johnny, you can't do that! Alice is our cousin! You can't marry your cousin!" He had capsized my mind in the short fifteen minutes he'd been there.

"We're getting married in Pomeroy next Saturday. It's far enough away, nobody will know. Don't you want to know why?" He finally focused his tear-filled eyes on me.

The deep hurt I saw brought my rant to a halt. "Yes," I almost whispered. "Why?"

"She needs to get out of that house." He sat on our log. "Awful things have been happening to her . . ."

We'd grown up around Alice. Their family always came to Kole doings. Never noticed any problems. Tom, feeling awkward in this private brother-sister conversation, went back to work. "Tell me." I sat by Johnny.

"In April, I lived with Aunt Maggie, Uncle Earl, and the girls in Clarkston while I looked for work. Slept on the floor. Didn't get much sleep. Didn't find a job.

"Something strange happened one night. A guy came knocking on the door after we'd gone to bed. Earl had been drinking as usual. He stumbled to open the door and almost stepped on me.

"This guy said, 'Half an hour,' and Uncle Earl answered with 'Two dollars.' Then the guy countered with, 'She's not worth two dollars. I'll give you one twenty-five.'

"I thought, *What's going on?* Uncle Earl got real huffy and told him it was one-fifty or leave. They argued back and forth till Earl told him to hand it over or get out. The man grumbled. I heard money clink and boots walk past me and down the hall."

"To where?" I asked, but my churning stomach already told me the answer.

"To Alice's room. He didn't even knock. Just walked in and shut the door. Muffled sounds came from the room. Then it got real quiet. Uncle Earl's chair scraped the kitchen floor. He walked down the hall, knocked, and said, 'Time's up.' The guy left without a word."

"Oh, Johnny. I never knew. She never said in any of her letters . . ." Earl worked construction so the family moved a lot: southern Idaho, back to Reubens, Oregon, back to Reubens, western Washington, back to Reubens, and now Clarkston. She wrote regularly, always sounding like she was having the time of her life.

Johnny continued, "I took her on a picnic the next day, had to get her alone. I point-blank asked her, 'Who was that guy last night?' She wouldn't answer. I insisted. Finally, she said it was one of her father's business partners. I kept pushing till she broke down crying and told me the whole story. Earl's been prostituting her to his friends since she was eight years old to get money for his booze." It was my turn to cry. "Now you see, Susie, why I have to marry her. It's her only way to escape."

"There must be some other way," I pleaded. "Doesn't she have friends? Couldn't she just run off with one of them?"

"No one." We sat in silence a long time. "I've got to get going. Wanted to tell you so you could help the folks understand. I already told Papa. Don't know how I'm going to tell Mama. Think I'll wait until after the fact. She'll be upset, but can't do anything about it."

He got up and headed to the car. "Oh, by the way, don't worry about our children. There won't be any. Some guy gave her a disease that took care of that." Trudging back to his little coupe, he climbed in and started up the hill to the farm.

I had just seen a whole different side of my brother.

Chapter 36

The Garden

Martha Zhalber sent her two oldest boys walking two miles uphill to our place with shovels and a note. "Susie, I heard you're wanting to make a garden. These boys will help you dig up a spot. Make sure they work hard." We'd already staked out where it would be. There was bear grass and some wild flowers but no stumps. I dreaded starting, remembering how rocky the ground had been, digging for the cabin. How nice of Martha, or, rather, her sons, to help. That's how it was then. If someone needed help, you send what help you could. Children were often the only commodity available during the Depression. With renewed excitement from the two big boys, I grabbed my shovel and announced, "It's out this way."

Clint put his shovel next to the stake and shoved down with his huge foot. Expecting to hear a grinding against rocks, I was amazed to see the curved metal slide cleanly into the dirt. "That can't be! It took us two months to dig the foundation for the cabin." I pushed my own shovel in. Not as smooth, but then, I only weighed ninety-eight pounds. If we had put the cabin on the east side of the hill instead of the west, digging would have been a breeze.

By noon, they turned over heaping shovels of rich black soil. I chose to follow along behind, knocking out the grass and picking out small stuff. We stopped for a drink, and they each pulled a sandwich out of their pockets. Martha had thought of everything.

"How's your folks doing?" I asked.

Clint swallowed, "Good, good. Pop's been hired at the granary this summer. It'll be a good steady job until the baby comes."

"Baby?"

"Yep," Clarence cleared his throat. "Number five."

"I didn't know that. How's your mama feeling?"

"Good, good," they chorused.

By mid-afternoon, they finished. "Thanks until you're better paid." It was embarrassing, not having anything to give them.

"Our privilege," Clarence said. "Hope we get to help out again. Uh, would you mind if I took some of those big worms out there? Would like to go fishing this afternoon in the creek."

I laughed, "Take all you want. Hope you catch enough for supper."

What nice boys. I hope Tom and I can raise children like that. I watched them head home, and my mind lingered on children. Two years and seven months we'd been married. When would we have our own? Tom wanted lots of babies. He was already an uncle to thirteen nieces and nephews who lived too far away to visit.

Having raised my sister Edna, my heart ached for my own baby. I imagined what it must be like to "be with child." At the same time, remembering how difficult giving birth was for Mama, it was scary. But she was old. In her forties. Goodness, she was old when she had me—thirty-eight. I'm not going to let that happen. We'll have lots of "kiddos" by the time I'm thirty. I laughed to myself thinking about that new word everyone seemed to call them—kiddos.

Tom returned from delivering fence posts around suppertime. "Only five more loads and we'll have enough to take a tree to the sawmill." He wore a grin. "Do you know what today is?"

"I have no idea." I'd long ago given up keeping track of days or dates. Time was measured by the sun, the moon, and the amount of work we accomplished.

"Think."

"I give."

"It's a day to celebrate."

"I know it's not my birthday. It's not warm enough yet."

"Nope. We've lived here one year!" He pulled a bouquet of wild flowers from behind his back and bowed as he gave them to me. "Congratulations to us." Our laughter mixed with difficult memories.

Some were buried, too hard to recall. The mind seals off those times too close to the incidents for the body to bear.

With the flowers decorating our small supper table, our talk turned to children. "What do you think our children will look like?" I looked at my handsome husband.

"Look like? Well, the boys will be handsome like me, and the girls will be as pretty as you." Tom's smile faded. "Seems strange we don't have any yet, doesn't it?"

Silence.

We continued to eat. I shouldn't have brought up the subject. Haven't you learned not to talk about things that make him look like a failure? I scolded myself. With seven children in his family, I'm sure he's wondering if the heavy work he had to do as a child or maybe the beatings are keeping him from being a father. The mood of celebration turned to moody. "I'm sure we'll have one soon," I ventured.

Silence.

"I'll tell you what—it's a good thing we don't have a baby yet. It wouldn't have survived this last year." At least Tom was thinking realistically.

"I completely forgot my surprise." I jumped up from the table, grabbed his hand, and pulled him to the newly spaded garden. "What do you think?"

"No! You did that while I was gone?" His smile was back. I was pleased that I'd managed to pull him out of his silence. I was learning.

"You didn't know you married such a powerful woman, did you?" I teased. I couldn't keep a straight face. "I must confess. I'm still just a weakling. Martha sent her two oldest boys to work it up. I paid them in worms."

Chapter 37

Raising the Roof

We fell into a summer routine. First thing in the morning, we'd cut down two trees. After dinner, I tended to the garden while Tom stripped branches and bark, then I helped cut them into posts. Some days, we'd do an extra tree. Around the first of August, Tom announced, "I think we've got enough saved to get the boards cut. I'm gonna ride to the mill and haggle with them."

Finally, I could see an end of tent living. Grabbing our little scythe, I mowed down the growth inside the house walls. We wouldn't have a floor this winter, but the grass was thick and we'd use the tent on the floor under our bed and table to keep the cold out. We would use leftover roof pieces to make a door. It had to go into place before we could finish the wall above it. No windows. Just as well. Warmer without windows. My imagination was running wild about what my house was going to look like. So big, we could have a dance in here, if we had a floor. Maybe someday?

"Susie! You here?" the mailman called. "Got a letter here from your mama."

I stepped out of the walls. "I was just cutting the floor," I laughed.

"Sure am proud of you kids sticking it out. Gonna have a real nice place to live this winter. Gotta get on home."

I tore open Mama's letter.

Dear Susie,

I just wanted to let you know we had a little accident coming home from Lewiston last night. We're all right. Edna has a few bumps and bruises. Papa hit his ribs on the steering wheel and I hit my head so I've got a headache this morning. The car lights went out coming up the hill. We decided we could use a flashlight to see. It wasn't very bright. Papa couldn't see the edge of the road and went over the bank. Wasn't very steep. We pushed the car back onto the road and waited till it got light to come on home. Didn't want you to hear what happened from someone else.

Love, Mama

Life is uncertain. I looked at Mama's signature, "Love, Mama." It took so long to win that love. I could have lost her last night. I sat there for a while thanking God for keeping my family safe.

I picked beans in the afternoon. Canned most of them, storing away for winter. Cooked a few for supper. We'd been enjoying lettuce, carrots, peas, beets, and beans. Papa had sent some seed potatoes, but they were just blooming, not ready to dig yet. My first garden was filled with life and hope.

Tom arrived with a string of fish. Winchester has a lake. One end of the lake is used to float logs until they're ready to cut. The other end is used for fishing. Five pan-sized trout dangled on the line in his hand. He cleaned them, I put some butter in a pan, and we feasted on the best fish I'd ever eaten.

Tom finished off his plate. "Well, you want to hear the good news?"

"The good news? What did they say?"

"The mill will rip five trees into boards for two dollars each."

"Two dollars? I thought they said three dollars last spring. You must have done some good dickering." I smiled. I could tell Tom wasn't finished.

"And—they will buy every tree we cut down, stripped, and debarked for a dollar apiece!"

"All the trees we can cut down? This whole fifteen acres?" Unbelievable.

He still wasn't finished, "And—they have a truck that will come once a week and haul the trees to the mill."

"People are really needing that much lumber?" I looked at our cabin, wondering about people struggling in these hard times in the city.

"Got to remember, we live a long way from the other side of the States. Not as bad here. It's tight, but the mill thinks business will bounce back quick." Tom was cautiously excited. "The downside is, if building stops, our deal is off."

"Then we'd better get cracking tomorrow."

In a week, our roof logs were hauled away.

We downed one of the beautiful cedar trees. Lodgepole wouldn't work for shakes. It grew straight, but the grain rounded the tree too tight. Tom sawed the cedar into short lengths and explained, "Now this is how ya make shakes. Grab her with your left, gently hit it on the other side with the hatchet, give it a hard bounce on the cutting block, and it'll split straight down." I remembered Grandma Kole telling how she'd split shingles for their first house. Tom made it sound so simple. Sure enough. A tap at the top, pick it up and bring it down hard, and there it was—a shingle. This might be fun.

We sold enough logs to buy tar paper and nails. We were prepared to raise the roof come the end of harvest. Family, friends, and even strangers swarmed over our house with noisy hammers and saws, which made visiting near impossible. Even Blacky had a part, pulling on the rope to lift the rafters. We had dinner with delicious covered dishes. By late afternoon, it was complete. The door with bright shiny hinges and a doorknob completed the picture.

I expected people to head home before supper. They went to their cars, returned bringing all kinds of instruments, marched right into our log house, and began to play. I lit the kerosene lamp, and Tom moved our little table into our new home. Our first piece of furniture held the lamp that lit the whole house. It was the best housewarming ever. Singing echoed in the hills until way after dark.

Our guests drifted away, and the music stopped too late to move the bed. Only one more night sleeping in the stinky tent. We might even be able to get a real mattress before winter.

Chapter 38

An Unexpected Guest

We did it! The late fall allowed enough time to cut a mattress worth of trees, plus two chairs and winter food for us and the animals. Kerosene was an important purchase. Without our lamp's light, it was pitch-black inside even in the middle of the day. We closed off the three-sided lean-to and made a barn to shelter our animals. What a great winter this would be.

Winter did what it always does. It brought wind, cold, and snow. We tucked ourselves, bearably warm, inside our snug walls. With such a large cabin, our winter's dry wood supply was stored inside. The shaved cedar kindling made fast starts to warm our mornings. The cold of last year became a distant nightmare. I sewed small cloth pouches, stuffed them with aromatic cedar needles, and hung them 'round the walls to freshen the air in our tightly enclosed room.

We were startled by pounding on the door during breakfast in late February. Tom reached for his gun and slid the lock out of place. Pounding came again, only lighter. He cracked the door far enough to reveal the silhouette of a large man against the dawn light.

"It's Friend! Let him in!" Why was he pounding on our door? He never visited our cabin; only stopped for coffee when we were outside working. The answer came at the sight of a gash on his forehead gushing red down his face. I grabbed dish towels while Tom helped him to a chair. Filling the cloths with snow, I pressed it against the cut just as Friend passed out.

"Get him on the old tic!" Tom yelled. We pulled the massive man little by little to the old mattress we'd saved—just in case. I held the cloths tight against the cut, hoping to stop the stream of blood. He began to shiver. We covered him with the bear skin he'd given us as a gift after we moved into the cabin. There was little else we could do.

The ooze of blood trickled to drops then seemed to seal itself off. A nasty bump began to rise, needing more cold presses. The shivering calmed, and Friend began to breathe normally.

"Got to feed the animals," Tom ran out the door, leaving it open for fresh air. My stomach threatened to rebel. I breathed in the invigorating cold.

Friend's eyes fluttered open as Tom came through the door and reached for his rifle. "Looks like we've got a wolf out there. Must have spooked Friend's horse right where the big rock is just north of the barn. Blood's all over the snow. No sign of the horse." He disappeared. I shut the door, thankful for the safety of walls for both us and the animals.

Friend tried to sit up but flopped back, holding his head, moaning. I lifted his head enough to give him a sip. He was out again. Waiting seems endless when you're in high anxiety. Where was Tom? What if he didn't get the wolf, but the wolf got him? If he slipped and fell, he'd be wolf dinner for sure. Wolves didn't come into this area often. In all my growing-up years, I'd only seen one. He was old and hungry and tried to attack our chickens. Browny, our dog, raised an awful fuss. Papa took that wolf down on the first shot.

There was no shot here—yet. Wait, wait, wait. I put snow packs on Friend's knot. Wait, wait, wait. Friend began muttering. What was he saying? Must be Nez Perce. Wait, wait, wait. I sent my silent request up to God, *Keep my Tom safe, please.* A single shot echoed across the hills. Did he get him? Still more waiting.

When Tom opened the door, he motioned for me to step outside. On the snow-covered log bench draped a gray hairy body with huge white fangs. No wonder the spooked horse threw his rider. A whine came from out by the barn. Tom went to check, and I returned to my patient.

It was five days before Friend could sit up on his own. We fed him spoons of water, soup, and coffee, graduating to mashed potatoes and oatmeal to help him gain strength. Not his regular diet, I'm sure. The afternoon of the sixth day, we heard voices outside. "Go," Friend spoke for the first time. "*Qaacii'yewyew* (*katsee yow yow*)." He extended his hand. Tom grasped it and smiled. "You're welcome."

The big man walked slowly to where his friends held his horse. After speaking with them for some time, they rode down the snowy dirt road. We didn't have another visit from the tribe until spring.

The snow melted, the ground thawed, and I began preparing our garden bed for planting. What's that sound? Horses, lots of horses clopping up the muddy, single-lane road from Culdesac. Tom heard too and stopped peeling bark. Headdresses appeared first up over the hill, followed by brown faces, and last, the Appaloosas they were riding. So many, we were overwhelmed and a little frightened. We stood in front of our cabin door and watched as more and more appeared. Men, women, and children halted their steeds around the area of our old tenting spot.

They spread grass mats on the flat area and began to load them with all sorts of unidentifiable foods. What was happening? Obviously, we weren't in immediate danger. Friend came out of the crowd with wide strides. He stood tall and hearty, extended his hand to Tom, and spoke one word, "Potlatch." He motioned for us to come. We followed and were surrounded by beautiful, smiling people.

Friend spoke slow and steady in Nez Perce, motioning around the area. He reenacted the story of last winter's accident to the silent, respectful audience. "Qaacii'yewyew. Come, eat," he pointed. It was then we realized his family and friends had dressed in their finest and provided this meal to say "Thank you for helping our brother." Potlatch—a party. There was feasting, laughing, and much nodding of the head. A drum began to beat a rhythm hard to resist. Everyone was soon pulled into the dance circle, even Tom.

Chapter 39

Alice's Deception

With soaring spirits and many friends' support, we disciplined ourselves into a routine that would take us to our goal. People often stopped and checked our progress. We installed one window in the cabin to save on kerosene, laid a floor, bought a cookstove, another horse, and best of all, an old car. The mill was up and running full-bore, and the area was recovering. We would never have reached this point without the help of friends.

My folks had been fairly distant during the last three years. We spent Christmas with them and saw them at the Fourth of July picnics but seldom in between. My mind was goal centered and blocked out concern, thinking no news is good news. They would let me know if help was needed. Letters were regular, holding daily routine information and local gossip. I had no idea what was really happening.

I was picking beans one morning, when I heard a car drive up. "Who's this?" I said out loud. I didn't recognize the car. Alice climbed out. "Hello, Alice. I didn't know you had a new car. When did you learn to drive?" We hugged. "Have a seat." I pointed to our now two-log benches. "Would you like a cup of coffee?" She sat while I fetched her a cup. "How good to have you visit. How's your folks?"

Her eyes sparked, "How's the folks? How's the folks? That's all I ever hear! Why doesn't anyone ever ask me how I am?" I was shocked into silence. What is going on? She took a sip of the coffee and continued, "That old lady's driving me insane. She follows me everywhere pretending to work, but I can feel her eyes poking me. She condemns me every chance she gets, 'Well if you hadn't . . . If you didn't . . . Can't you do anything right? You've ruined my son's life. Be careful, you big, clumsy oaf.' I'm about ready to flip." Stunned, I found no words to offer.

"If I'd known I was gonna have to live with that old witch, I would never have married Johnny. He's such a mama's boy that he . . ."

"What?" I broke in, "You're living with my folks?"

Hatred shot from her eyes. "Nobody told you, did they? Nobody has the guts to talk about the shame—the shame of who I am and what I've lived with. Shame of why Johnny married me and his shame of not being able to make a living. It's shame, shame, shame on the whole Kole family."

I repeated, "You're living with my folks?"

"Nine months. Cooped up in that house all winter with that old bat, a spoiled rotten kid, and two men who're beaten down by that controlling woman."

"I didn't know." What else could I say?

"Johnny's beaten to a pulp. She controls his every move. Never a moment, I mean never a moment are we left alone. He cries all night. She even told me when we first got there, I could sleep in your room. I refused. What right does she have to control our marriage? I'm sick and tired of it. If I had a gun, I'd shoot all of them; Johnny and I would run away where no one could find us and we'd be happy forever."

I kept quiet although my mind was screaming, No! No! This can't be happening to my family!

"She's got this list every day. It has to be done or we don't get supper. We're slaves. She treats us like children. She's mean and manipulative. It's her way or no way. If it weren't for Johnny's father intervening, she'd have kicked us out long ago. Where would we go? We don't have no money, no job. Johnny hates farming."

Alice stopped long enough for me to ask, "What happened to the Fuller Brush job?"

"Nobody has money to spend on that kind of stuff. Johnny tried. He really tried. Three whole months, he went door to door peddling. A peddler, mind you! Not a decent job. Didn't even earn enough to pay rent, let alone buy food. We had to get poor man's food in the soup line to survive. How degrading! Embarrassing! He quit! Couldn't find anything else. Jobs are still scarce in Lewiston, at least ones that don't need training. Got a couple of house repair jobs. That's hard work. He's not strong, you know. Came home exhausted every night."

My heart sank. That meant no payback to the folks for buying the business starter kit. That also meant no money for planting crops this year. Mama and Papa's world was being turned upside down. What was going to happen to the farm?

I looked out toward the road. "Nice car. When did you get that?"

"Today. I rode down to Lewiston with Uncle Ope to pick it up." Her attitude suddenly turned happy.

My mind was chasing its tail. If they're broke, couldn't afford to live on their own, had to move in with the folks, where did the money come from for this car? All I could say was, "Oh."

"I came by to tell you we're leaving for California. We're done putting up with slavery. We're declaring our freedom. Johnny's gonna have everything packed by the time I get back. He's gonna stand up and be a man. We're throwing it all in the car and leaving. Thought it would be right for me to stop and tell you. You've always treated me decent."

"Thanks," I replied, looking down to hide the tears. After years of living with Mama's rejection and Johnny's meanness, I understood that my relationship with my family was about to change.

Alice climbed back in her fancy new car, smiled viciously, and waved, "Bye, We're gonna be free and happy."

As she drove away, I collapsed on the log. Why does everything have to be so complicated? Where's the loving, tight-knit farm family you hear about? Why can't people get along, understand, and accept each other? My life had been torn apart again by uncontrollable sadness. What have we done wrong, God? I heard a soft rustling in the grass. With a quick glance, I spied a snake making his way into hiding.

Chapter 40

Heartbreak on the Homestead

After sharing the California news, Tom insisted that I go visit the folks for a few days. We felled as many trees as possible the next day, so Tom could keep working, then he drove me to the farm. I dreaded facing them. What was I going to say? Tears flowed, and my small, white handkerchief was soaked by the time we got there. Not knowing what to say, Tom gave me a kiss, a hug, and said, "I'll come back on Monday to pick you up."

The place was quiet—like the calm before the storm when even birds hush their singing. The whole earth was holding its breath with me. I managed to make my feet move toward the house.

As I stepped on the porch, the screen door banged open and Edna grabbed me, "I knew you'd come. I can always count on you." I held my grown-up fifteen-year-old sister tight as she sobbed hysterically on my shoulder. We sat on the steps. When she was all cried out, she shuddered. "It's like living in a morgue."

I looked around. No horses, no cow in the barn, no chickens in the pen, no pig. "Where are the animals?"

"Been butchered or sold," Edna sighed.

"Just that quick?" How fast things were changing.

"Nope. That's what we've been living on since last fall. Takes a lot to feed five grown-ups. Can't believe how much Alice can eat. She can go through one ham all by herself if you'd let her. No wonder she's such a big cow."

"Edna . . ." I began to scold.

"Had to sell the horses to buy food for the cow but finally had to sell the cow too."

We went to Grandmama's for Christmas dinner. The folks came to the Stick Ranch to visit a few times, but I hadn't been to the farm for over a year. Now I understood why they always made arrangements to see us someplace else. They'd been selling off the farm piece by piece, animal by animal, just to survive. They kept it a secret from me.

"What happens now?"

"Don't know. Papa found out this morning that the crop money he'd been storing away to buy a place in Lewiston is gone. He went to town to put up farm auction signs for next Saturday. Mama's in bed. The auction's the last straw for her."

The new car! Now I knew where the money came from for the new car. How could they do that to the people who had taken them in, given them a place to sleep, and food out of their own barn? Did the folks know that? How could I ask without raising suspicion?

"Uh, where's Johnny and Alice?" I inquired naively.

"Don't know. Haven't seen them since Thursday. Sure like it when they're gone. Quiet and peaceful. They left a note saying they went to town with friends. We were in Reubens visiting Aunt Juna."

Oh, my goodness. Could this get any worse? It was Aunt Juna's husband, Uncle Ope, who had taken Alice to Lewiston to get the new car. Was the whole family in on this conspiracy?

"Uh, Edna, can you keep a secret?"

"Ya-ah."

"Promise you won't say anything until I tell you." That had her attention. She nodded. I took a deep breath. "Johnny and Alice won't be coming back . . . they uh . . . left on Thursday to go, uh, to go to California . . ."

"What?" Edna yelled. I shushed her.

"They went to California to start a brand-new life." I finished quickly.

Edna's blue eyes stared at me. She shook herself like a dog shaking off water, "Well, good riddance!"

"Don't say that. It's going to break Mama's heart. Johnny's always been special to her."

"Until he married Alice. You can't imagine what it's been like. Screaming, yelling, throwing things, silence, crying, banging doors. It's been a loony bin. Mama will be glad they're gone."

Papa came putt-in' up in the old Model T. "Remember, you promised not to say anything," I warned Edna.

He climbed slowly out and walked toward the house like he was carrying a sack of rocks on his back. He shuffled along, looking at me with eyes that had turned out the light. "Sorry, Susie. Thought we could do it. Lost it all. We've lost everything."

My arm went around his waist as we walked into the bare house. All that remained was the dining table, four chairs, cookstove, and Mama's little rocking chair. The bare living room held only my phonograph and Papa's chair. I pictured my wedding in that room, full of chairs, people, laughter, and happiness. Another piece of me that was no longer going to exist. Memories of smells, sights, and sounds would be all I could hang on to. Change eats away at the heart, and I must decide what to do with this.

Mama came down the stairs. "Is it set for Saturday?" Her dull voice echoed in the emptiness. Papa nodded. "Susie . . ." I hugged my mama. She needed me to hug her, but I needed even more for her to hug me. I must know that the love I worked so hard to earn was still in her. "Susie, we're leaving. Too old to work land. No help. No seed money . . ." She sat in her little chair, her own emotions rocking to the rhythm of her falling tears.

"Papa, can I talk to you for a minute?" I motioned toward the porch. "I'd like to see the barn again." I wanted to get far enough away so Mama couldn't hear. Standing on the straw-covered floor, I cleared my voice, "Papa, I need to tell you that Johnny and Alice are gone. They won't be coming back. They left for California. Thought Johnny could get a job there." There was no change of expression on his face. "Alice came by the cabin and told me."

"I know where they've gone and I know how they're gettin' there." Papa's voice cracked. "It's a chicken's way out. Took the savings, bought a car, left a horrible note . . ."

"What note? Edna told me the note said they had gone to town with friends."

"Oh, that note. It was an old one. I traded it for the one I destroyed. The one full of hateful, mean things would've killed your mother. Can't lose my son and my wife too."

Chapter 41

The Auction and Beyond

I sent a hastily written note to Tom by the mailman on Saturday, hoping he'd read it before Monday. I urged Mr. Denton to put it directly in his hands. "It's extremely important." I was telling my husband the quick version of the auction, moving, and how I needed to stay until the sale was over. I knew he'd understand.

A farm auction's like a giant rummage sale. Edna and I helped Papa move equipment in a row so it could be examined easier. We put planks on sawhorses and laid tools from the barn in a neat row. Papa put a few in the back of the truck he thought he might need on a new place. From the house, we brought two beds, dressers, washstands, buckets, anything that probably wouldn't be useful in the city.

I helped box up books, pictures, clothes, bedding, dishes, and pots and pans. My phonograph would go home with me when Tom came. The rest was put in the yard for auction. The cast iron cookstove and the telephone on the wall would be sold with the house. What scary memories those held for me when the lightning had flashed across the room.

Come Friday, we loaded the folks' bed in the pickup. Uncle Jim came with a wagon and loaded the other furniture.

We spent the night sleeping on the floor. This floor, I thought, how many times did I scrub this floor on my hands and knees from the time I was six? Scrubbing had been my job. I made a game of it, naming each board by its color, pattern, and size. That one in the middle was

Mighty Little Mountain. A short little board with a mountain-shaped woodgrain, it was walked *on continuously, making it mighty strong. My game extended into talking to each piece. "Good to see you today, Miss Tall Brown. Where have you been to get so dirty?"* This floor taught me to make light when life hands you a tough row to hoe. I reached out my hand and ran it over the worn, smooth wood. I had one more thing to say, *Thank you.*

Up at sunrise, I laid out bread, apricots from the tree, some raspberries, and butter. A strange meal, but it satisfied our hunger. The auction was set for nine o'clock to give farmers time to get chores finished. Life moved a little faster now with vehicles. The first potential buyers started arriving a half hour early. Mostly men. Some brought their wives, and a couple of young farmers even their children. Sometimes at auctions there would be refreshments, but this hardship sale wouldn't have any. The auctioneer began right at nine. No dillydallying. Farmers were busy people in summer. It was hard to hear items selling for mere pennies of what they cost. I glanced at Papa. He was nodding, even smiled once in a while. Mama's blank expression gave no clues about her feelings.

The farm itself was the last to sell. Mama had homesteaded it over forty years ago. This would be the hardest to release. Three men earnestly bid. That was good. It meant the price would go higher. The bidding slowed as each man mentally calculated the cost versus the value of the future crops. One dropped out, leaving two dueling to the end. One hundred fifty acres plus a two-story, five-bedroom house, large barn, chicken coop, pig pen, orchard, and large garden plot sold for one thousand five hundred and fifty-five dollars. The auctioneer banged his gavel, and the sale was finished. It seemed a good price considering the times.

There was a collective sigh from all four of us. It was enough. Enough to buy a new place in Lewiston and start over. Farmers and families came to say goodbye, giving their well wishes. These forever friends shared good times and hard times through many years.

The dust along the road announced a car arriving, which held the man I loved. He loaded the phonograph in the trunk. "Looks like we'll be hearing music," he remarked. "Edna, you ride with us. We're going to Lewiston and help unload."

Mama looked sharply at Tom. "We don't have no place to unload," she scowled.

Papa put a hand on Mama's shoulder. "Oh, I forgot to tell you. Tom and I bought ten acres and the old water office building in the Lewiston Orchards last Thursday. It's just sitting there waiting for us to move in." Both men were grinning ear to ear.

Chapter 42

Baby Silence

With Mama, Papa, and Edna semi-settled in their new home, Tom and I put all the energy we could muster into the remaining trees. Four years of survival have passed. There never could be one as bad as the first year. Each year progressed in comfort, but it never felt like home. Four years of sawing, cutting, and debarking. We'd become proficient by this time. The question is, with only one year left to fill our contract, could we make the deadline? The remnant of two acres was downhill, making it more difficult to move the logs to the pickup site. What would happen if we didn't finish? I giggled at the thought. Would they just kick us out? No matter. Our five years would be up. The worst would be a demand for rent. How much would that be?

The subject of babies kept popping up as friends stopped to visit. Everyone seemed to be expecting. Katherine was the first. They'd been married for five years. Delmar could talk of nothing except, "When the baby comes, we'll . . ." Katherine was glowing. She chattered about the things she was crocheting for the baby, the bed that Delmar had made for the baby, the quilt our grandmama had made for the baby. The baby, the baby, the baby! Every expectant couple was totally wrapped up in "the baby." Each time they went on their way, I endured many days of Tom silence.

Isn't it interesting how blind we can be to others' feelings when good things are happening to us? It's a devastation of the heart. Those families had no idea the deep hurts their "baby excitement" caused us. Was this hurt of our own making? Maybe we suffered because we never shared our own longing for a baby. We were afraid to say it out loud and have everyone feel sorry for us. Pity is a dreadful thing to endure. It's on the edge of toppling over into shame. Tom and I were quite the pair. Neither of us expressed our own thoughts or needs. Our childless situation after six years of marriage had driven a strong, unspoken wedge between us.

What could I do but pray like Hannah. I tried to convince myself I wasn't the only childless woman who ever lived. Digging out my Bible, I reread the story of Hannah. She was desperate for a child, like me. She was mocked because she had no children, like me. Mine was a mocking of my own making. She begged God to open her womb, like me. She prayed and wept in anguish, like me. She promised to give her child back to the Lord—unlike me. "No, Lord, I couldn't possibly give up my child. Hannah was a far stronger woman than me." I would have to chew on this thought.

Silence. That's the problem at hand. I must find a way to pull Tom back, divert him away from thinking he's a failure. I changed my strategy and tried the chatter technique again. Every morning, I greeted my husband with a kiss, a smile, and small talk. "I found a patch of wild strawberries yesterday. I'll go pick some for supper after we get the trees cut. The green beans are doing well. Much better than last year. I'm going to collect some of the pitch and save it. I heard it can be used for medicine . . ." I go on and on, only to be met by silence.

Tom made the trip to the spring every other day for fresh water. Once a month, he went to town to stock up on supplies. The car certainly made that easier. He never invited me to go along. Looking at my worn-out, faded dresses, I certainly understood. They were at least two sizes too big. If it hadn't been for my apron tied firmly around my waist, I believe they would have just slipped off. What a sight I must be. I hadn't seen myself in a full-length mirror since we lived in Clarkston. Thank goodness for the small pair of sewing scissors that I painstakingly used to keep my hair short. There was no time to fuss with beauty of the body out in the woods.

On October 1, Tom came home with the winter supplies for us and the animals. He also brought bullets for the rifle. "What's this?" I asked.

"What's it look like?" He threw back. "Going huntin' so we'll have meat."

"You bought a hunting license? Deer or elk?"

"Are you daft, woman? I could never bring down an elk with this little pea shooter." He picked up the gun and walked out the door. Later, I heard the *bam, bam* of target practice.

I spent the rest of the afternoon squirreling away the supplies. "Lord, help him have a successful hunt. He needs to succeed at something right now."

Chapter 43

Christmas of '34

It was a mild winter. If we could make it to the main highway, roads might be clear for us to go to the folks for Christmas. Snow in Lewiston was always lighter because of the low elevation of seven hundred feet.

"Could we go a day early so I could do some gift-shopping?" I dared ask one morning.

"I s'pose." He smiled at me. "Write Neen. See if we could stay at her place."

His sister, Neva, had married a man twenty-two years her senior. Otis was a tiny, quiet man. He owned ten acres in the Orchards where he raised produce. They never had children. It would be a safe place away from baby conversation. "Maybe they wouldn't even mind if we stayed until New Year's and we could go back to our holiday tradition," I ventured.

"Could be. I'll see if one of the Zhalber boys would milk Bessy and feed the horses. I'm sure they could use the milk with all those young-uns." They had added two in the last four and a half years.

With winter approaching, our expectant family members and friends visited less and the mood in our home became lighter. Our spirits were high as the holidays approached. I made a shopping list for my family. It was easy to think of things since they'd given up so much last spring. Edna loved to draw. I saw colored pencils in a catalogue. I hoped they had them in the stores. Mama lost one of her favorite blue earrings. I'd look for another pair that matched the color of her eyes.

Papa dropped his pocket watch, and he'd been living on "sun time." Tom. What to get Tom? A gift needed to be something from me. If I bought him something, it would be from our money, not from me. I'd have to think about this.

Originally, the water office, which now served as home to the folks, had one long room for people to come in and pay bills, with three smaller rooms for the office workers. Someone had remodeled it into a house. They created a living room from the reception area, cut an arch into the end office for a dining room, another arch into the next office for a kitchen, and then kept the doors on the adjoining room for a bedroom. The front door held a cut-glass panel of a magnificent elk. The only other building was an outhouse about one hundred feet from the backdoor.

Papa spent the summer digging a root cellar next to the house and building a screened porch over it. On one side of the porch, he made a door on the floor with stairs leading down to shelves lined with jars of vegetables and fruit from the summer garden. The Transparent Apple tree next to the house had provided gallons of applesauce. The old cherry tree in the middle of the grassy field yielded many jars of deep, red Bings. They would have food for winter.

With only one bedroom, Edna slept on the davenport in the living room. That meant she had to get up early every morning before going to school, fold up her blankets, and turn it into a sitting room. Being a teenager, she hated everything. Letter after letter she raged on and on. "The school is too big, I'll never make friends here. The school work's too hard. The teachers expect me to know too much. The first day of school, I got off the bus at the wrong corner and was walking in the horrid heat when Aunt Grace and Belledene came along and gave me a ride home. It was so embarrassing. I have to ride a smelly, old bus to school then walk a mile when I get home. Everybody teases me. Can I please come live with you?" As much as my heart wanted to rescue her, I knew it couldn't be. She would find a way. We all find our own way to survive.

Neen welcomed us with open arms. Since they had only one bedroom, we slept on her Daveno. How convenient this invention was! You grab under the front seat and lift it. It would tip into a V shape. By pushing it further, a lock released then you pull it toward you and it flattens into a double bed. This was definitely something on my list of furniture, if we ever get a home of our own.

We were on Lewiston's main street as soon as the stores opened. With a twinkle in his eye, Tom gave me money with orders, "Don't spend it all in one place." While he visited some friends he bumped into, I slipped off to explore on my own with a promise to meet at Montgomery Ward in an hour and a half. I filled the list for my family within an hour. I was pleased. Now, Tom. Many new items lined the counters of the stores. My isolation for four and a half years on the Stick Ranch left me behind. I was fascinated by the men's new-styled hats. Wouldn't Tom look handsome in a gray front-peaked felt-brimmed hat? Never mind that he couldn't wear it on the ranch. We wouldn't be there forever. It wasn't something he would buy for himself. I had enough to buy it and still have two dollars left. Hmm, what size? The clerk looked about Tom's size. I inquired. He demonstrated. I bought. He even wrapped it discreetly so it didn't look like a hat. What a surprise! My heart was full and happy. We stopped at the grocery store and bought a ham for Christmas dinner with the last two dollars.

It was a peaceful Christmas Day. We ate till we were stuffed, washed up the dishes, then gathered in the living room to open gifts. Mama embroidered a new set of flour sack dish towels for us. Edna painted a picture that Papa framed. Everyone was delighted with my choice of gifts for them. The only one missing was Johnny. No one spoke of him, but his absence was very present.

I saved my gift for Tom until last. It became his most prized possession, always crowning his head when he headed to town.

Chapter 44

River, Stay Away from My Door

The snow left early and we tackled the last of the trees with gusto. We had paid back the thirty-five dollars we borrowed that first year of survival. We bought an old car, a used cookstove, a real bed, table and chairs, and had plenty to eat. Yes, we had made it through the Great Depression and even saved a little money.

The anticipated letter from the government came the last week of May. "Thank you for clearing this plot of land. We appreciate your service. You will need to vacate this property by June 15, 1935." Blood, sweat, and tears had been endured here. We'd have to sell the animals. It was a bittersweet leaving.

Tom put out feelers for work, knowing we'd soon have to move. The Kerbys were the most promising employers. They owned a dairy called Cherry Lane Ranch. He went to see them the day after our notice came and was hired.

Now the question was, where to live? Tom's parents had sold their farm at Clearwater the year before. They rented the largest of three houses along the Clearwater River between the Lewiston Lumber Mill and Spaulding. The two houses next to them were empty. Tom moved us next to my much-feared father-in-law! The distance was shorter to the dairy, but I was isolated from main traffic, telephones, and safety. High anxiety hounded me. How could Tom think of doing this to me? He knew how much I lived in fear of his father.

Paris, Tom's youngest brother, was sixteen and still lived at home. He worked in Lewiston. Frankie and her husband, Walt, temporarily moved in with their baby until a construction job opened up in Portland. With five adults and a baby girl living in the big house, Mother Chase was delighted to have so many of her family living around her. However, no one had the nerve to rebuke Tom's father when he said suggestive things to me. Thank goodness Paris came to my rescue and quickly removed me from the situation. My grandma's voice echoed, *Be nice to others and they'll be nice to you.* My mind fought back, *but this man wants me to be nice to him so he can destroy me. I can't do it.*

Coming from cool mountain summers to unbearable valley heat was a shock to our systems. The sun's glare bounced off the racing water, bringing extra misery. Mother Chase had started a garden on the easy sloping bank of the Clearwater River. Mornings were consumed with carrying buckets of water from the river to the top of vegetable rows and pouring it into ditches. It seemed futile to me. The sandy ground with small rocks protruding everywhere gobbled the water before it flowed halfway. She insisted it worked last year.

The first months went well. Tending the garden and cleaning the house that sat empty for months kept me occupied. I managed to avoid confrontation with Tom's father. "Tom's father." That's all I could call him. Everything else seemed undeserving: Father, Papa, Dad? No, he had to earn those titles. He would be "Tom's father."

I was expected to visit the big house each day. If I didn't, they thought I was upset about something and would send Paris over. "Uh, everyone wants to know what you're mad about," he would say. "You didn't get over to the big house today." They didn't seem to understand that I needed to be alone and wanted to be busy in my own house. After all, I lived the past five years in near solitude.

I barely had time to correspond with my own folks. I wrote a little each day. Neen came to visit her family two times a week and took a letter to my folks in the Orchards on her way home. Mama sent letters back when Neen made the return trip. I had no time to be lonely. I was excited to read their letters and hear how things were going in their new place. I hoped they were being honest with me. I sent letters to other family members with Neen to be mailed in our box five miles away by the lumber mill. The cost of two cents a letter was worth it. No one writes to you unless you write to them. Paris stopped on his way home from work to pick up the mail.

Winter hit fiercely that first year down by the riverside. Temperatures plummeted to thirty-five degrees below zero. Even the old rooster's comb froze, and Mother Chase had to bring him inside, along with five laying hens.

She came one evening to see how Tom's sore throat was. "What's that sound I hear?" She went into the kitchen and discovered a frozen pipe broken under the sink. Water was pumped up to the houses from the river, and our entire line was frozen. Our water supply was gone. We'd have to get water from the big house or melt ice from the river.

In two days, the entire river froze over so deep, you could walk all the way across on it. That crazy kid, Paris, did that—just to say he did.

Five days later, I wrote to the folks:

"*The river, or rather the ice, sure has been breaking today, cracklin' and poppin'. Boy! It sounds like a giant with arthritis, yawning and getting up from his nap. We can see it piled on up the river a ways. When it melts, Neen and I'll sing and sing, 'River Stay 'Way from My Door.' It's pushed the mill logs right up on the bank. Tom, Paris, and Walt are using log chains to pull them on up to the house for firewood and building fences.*"

Four days later, the thaw caused the river to rise a foot. By the end of the next week, the water rushed by three feet from our backdoor.

Chapter 45

The Nightmare

My worst nightmare came the next summer when Mother Chase left to visit Frankie in Portland. She would be gone one month. Paris now worked in road construction and moved out. The garden was my responsibility. It wasn't that I wanted to shirk my duty. I could carry the water, I could weed. I was a hard worker, but I was overwhelmed by how I was going to do all that with nowhere to run, nowhere to hide when left alone with Tom's father, the only other human being in this deserted place.

He drove Mother Chase to the train station early in the morning. He didn't come home that day or the next or the next. I guessed he found a lady friend, but of course, I had no proof. Each day, I hauled water like mad, hoping to get done before he returned. Each night, I lay awake, wondering if tomorrow would be the day.

"Tom, is there a key to this house?" I questioned on the third day.

"S'pect any skeleton key would fit that lock," he answered. There was no more discussion. A skeleton key? It was long, skinny, and had two prongs on the end. One key would open any lock. Even if I had a skeleton key, so would my father-in-law. What good would it do? A key wasn't the answer.

About eight o'clock on the evening of the fourth day, the disturbing sound of a car coming from the direction of Lewiston rumbled up the narrow dirt road. He was coming. What would I do? Tom would be home in an hour after evening milking. A lot could happen in an hour. I rushed into the house, closed all the windows and doors, pulled a dresser in front of the backdoor, and shoved the second-hand settee against the front door. Sitting on the floor, I listened and prayed as the house grew dark with the setting sun. Crickets were the only sound.

The creaking of the door to his house caused me to scramble into the darkest corner and curl in a fetal position. I counted, only to fifty, before the door opened again. The car door slammed, the house door again complained. What's going on? Has he brought someone else to the house? I almost wished he had.

The silence hurt my ears as I strained to hear sounds. Then it happened. The door opened and footsteps could be heard tramping through the dry grass. I held my breath, hoping he would think I'd left. A flashlight flickered through the window, stalking me as I huddled in the corner nearest the window. Heavy steps on the porch, then a sharp rap of knocks. Silence, then more persistent rapping. I had stopped breathing. My heart was in my throat.

"Susie? Are you home, Susie?" My ears couldn't understand the sounds. My mind wouldn't accept the voice. It wasn't a man's voice. It was the voice of Neen. "Yes," I squeaked. "Is that you, Neen?"

"Are you all right, Susie? You sound like you're sick? You don't have a light." She rattled the doorknob and tried to push in.

"Give me a minute." I began tugging the settee away from the door, opening it a crack to make sure she was alone. I saw her in the evening shadows with something in her hand. I flung open the door, never so glad to see anyone in my life. My hug was genuine. "I'm so glad it's you!"

"What's going on here?" She flashed the light around the room.

I shoved the settee into its proper place. "Have a seat. I'll light the lamp."

"Father went up to Stanley's for a few days. He'll be back day after tomorrow. I came to make sure the groceries were stocked up and put fresh water in the pail. He refuses to do woman work, but when he gets hungry enough, I bet he'll fix himself a bowl of cereal or else be coming over here for meals."

All I could respond with was, "Oh." It would have been kind to tell me so I didn't have to live in terror all these days.

"Now, tell me why you had the doors blocked and the lights out."

I poured out my heart to this woman I knew would understand. She listened then quietly responded. "Oh, Susie. I know your fear. Been there myself. Remember, I lived with him for seventeen years and finally married Otis to escape his abuse. I couldn't take it any longer. He's mean and selfish, a sick old man who can't control himself. I thought it was just us girls he tortured. How dare he go after you too. You're so good for my brother. Father was so mean to him all his life. I was surprised Tom wanted to live next to him. You know what, after Tom goes to work, I'll come down and stay with you. I won't let anything happen to you."

"What about Otis? Doesn't he need your help?"

"Otis was a bachelor for twenty years before he married me. He can take care of himself. He'll understand."

We heard Tom's old car coming up the road. I realized I hadn't even started his dinner. "Never mind." Neen got up. "I made a potpie for Father. I'll bring it over and we'll share it."

"Thank you." I looked at her with tears in my eyes. "Please, don't tell Tom any of this."

"It's our secret," she said as she stepped out the door. I hurried to set the table for three.

Chapter 46

Terror

My guardian angel, Neen, came every day. We worked together on the garden, cleaned both houses, cooked, and laughed together. Tom's father wouldn't speak, only grunted, nodded, or shook his head. The silent treatment! Now, I understood where the silent treatment came from when a situation couldn't be handled. Neen ignored him. I followed her example. He should have been happy to have a place to sleep, company, and good food on the table.

The Chases had moved off the farm when all the children married or left. It was too much work for broken-down bodies in their late sixties. He would be seventy his next birthday. Stubborn as a mule. He refused to accept the fact that he was old. He used fear and aggression to control. No wonder his wife left for a month.

Two days before Mother Chase's return date, Neen didn't come. Panic seized me. Should I run away? No trees or bushes—no place to hide. The nearest house was three miles. Could I run that far? I couldn't swim, so the river wasn't an option.

Again, I barricaded myself in our house, shut the windows, pulled the shades, sat, and waited. It was dark, stifling hot, and suffocating. The thermometer reached one hundred ten degrees. On hands and knees, I pulled the water bucket with the dipper from the kitchen to where I crouched in the darkest corner of the living room. I made myself drink sparingly. I didn't know how long my supply had to last. I dozed now and then, waking with a start at every noise.

Fear does strange things when it takes over the mind. I began to see things, moving things, in the darkness of the house. Strange demon-like characters floated in and out of my hiding room. I sensed them grabbing and holding my arms and legs. When I forced my limbs to move, it was slow and jerky like in silent picture shows. My dry, swollen throat could barely swallow sips of water from the dipper. Dry eyes stared into the dimness. Blinking was painful. Was I going to live through this day?

Into this foreboding situation, a quiet voice spoke in my mind: "For God has not given us a spirit of fear, but of power and of love and of a sound mind." Yes, I remembered reading that someplace in the Bible. Fear has replaced my psaltery, weak faith, hobbling even my prayers. Was this evil real or a creation of my imagination?

A knock! "Susie, you've been hiding in this house all day. Come spend some time in the fresh air with me." It was him!

My mind shouted, "No! It's not my imagination."

"Come on, sweetie pie. It's just you and me. We need each other. Gets mighty lonely out here."

I remained silent.

"You probably want me to come in. A woman's always more comfortable in her own place."

Silence, silence, silence.

"I know you been wantin' a baby. That husband of yours is no good for stuff like that, you know. Fact is, he's no good for anything. What you ever saw in him's beyond me."

Silence!

"Come on, let me in. I can show you how to make real, good babies and lots of them."

Tears streamed down my hot cheeks, my eyes burned with fire. "God, where's my Neen angel?" I inquired silently.

I was shocked by the breaking glass in the bedroom. I moved with miraculous speed to slam the room's door and shove the table against it. Climbing in the window, he swore as he cut himself on the shards of broken glass. What now? I pulled the settee away from the front door enough to get the door open and slip out. I heard him pounding and shoving the bedroom door open. My stiff legs carried me to the empty house next door. As I shut the door, my hand felt a bolt on the inside. Sliding it in place, I dashed to the other door. Yes, there was one there. Better yet, I discovered a closet with a dead bolt on the inside. Not even questioning why it was there, I entered the tiny space, locked the door, lost my sense of balance in the pitch-black darkness and sat hard on the rough floor.

Silence. But only for a moment. I could hear Tom's father cussing, throwing things, pounding on walls, turning over furniture. What would be left of the precious few things we owned? The crashing and banging came to a stop. The door flew open with great force, splintering as he kicked it repeatedly. Silence. I knew, beyond a doubt, that if he ever caught me, his anger would result in my last breath.

I waited. I realized in that moment I had waited most of my life. Waited for Mama's acceptance, waited to grow up, waited to be good enough, waited to get married, waited for my husband's trust, waited for a real home, waited for a child—now, waiting for someone to save me. I fell asleep waiting.

The sound of a motor woke me. It was followed by a man yelling and screaming. *Where was I? Why was it so dark?* I tried to stretch. I couldn't even unfold my legs. In alarm, I began to feel the walls. My hands ran into spider webs and protruding nails. Then I remembered, I'm in a safe place—a shelter. Without my angel, Neen, God had given me protection.

"Where is she? What have you done with her?" Tom's shouts were followed by what sounded like a fist jab. "I'll beat the daylights out of you like you used to do to me if you've hurt her!" This time, a slap. "Tell me where she is!"

"I don't know." I heard Tom's father breathing hard in between words. "I—I never saw her."

I knew it must be getting dark if Tom was home. In mid-August, the days are getting shorter. I felt for the bolt and slipped it off. The dusky house allowed me to find my way to the backdoor and slip the second bolt. I felt an urgency to reach Tom before he killed his father. My wooden legs moved slowly toward the two of them in the back of the house.

"Stop, Tom. I'm here." I called. Tom whirled around, took three steps, and I collapsed, sobbing into his arms. "No more hitting, Tom. Please, no more hitting." As much as I feared his father, I had a strong reverence for life. Even cruel creatures have a right to live, with the possibility of change.

"I'm so sorry, Susie. I'm so sorry." He held me tight. I sobbed on his shoulder. My husband, my hero. A memory of Papa and chickens flashed through my mind. Yes, there is a man who loves me as much as the first man in my life.

Chapter 47

Aftermath

When he released me, Tom wasted no time forcing his father into the passenger seat of his own car and throwing some clothes and items into a bag. "I'll be back as soon as I deposit this so-and-so at Grace's. She can do whatever she wants with him. He'll never be back here!" He jumped behind the wheel and sped off.

I watched till the car was out of sight. "Thanks for sending my hero to save me. God, calm, my husband. That little narrow road's no speedway, not made for driving with out-of-control anger."

I ventured into our house. Disaster—total disaster. In his rage, Tom's father had not left one thing unturned. In the dim light, I began with the big items: righted the settee, the table with a broken leg, the chairs that seemed to be in one piece, the dresser drawers dumped all over the floor, and the one living room chair. What to do with the rest? It was too dark to see, but I had to keep moving. I grabbed my straw broom and began to sweep. I was relieved to hear Tom drive in. He still had his father's car. That meant there was no way he could come back. I was safe—at least for now.

"I called Neen while I was at Grace's," Tom shook his head. "She told me about coming every day to stay with you. I had no idea he'd been threatening you."

"I . . . I didn't want you to worry or get upset." Neen had told. Now, I would be the one to receive the silent treatment. Why did she break her promise? I had to ask, "Why didn't she come today?"

"Otis fell off the ladder this morning pickin' peaches. She had to take him to the hospital. He's gonna be all right. Just bruised up. Nothin' broken."

"Oh . . . I'm sorry."

It was dark now. Tom went to his car and got a flashlight, exposing the mess. He shook his head. "We can't stay here tonight. Let's go to Neen's. Tomorrow's my day off. We'll come clean up." We slowly walked out to the car in the trail of light. Each of us was lost in our own thoughts during the half-hour drive.

Next thing I knew it was nine o'clock in the morning. I woke to the smell of coffee and quiet voices in the kitchen. We'd slept in what we had on; hadn't brought a change of clothes. What a sight I must be. I ran my fingers through my hair then washed my face in the bowl next to the Daveno. Aw, that felt good. My stomach thundered, and I realized we hadn't eaten last night. I hadn't eaten since breakfast yesterday. The smell of bacon called from the kitchen, along with the sizzling of fried eggs and the flapping of pancakes being turned over.

Otis—Teddy, as Neen affectionately called him—sat at the end of the four-person table. He had a swollen eye and lip, and his arm in a sling. He gave me a brave smile when I came in. "Good morning," he whispered. I could tell it was an effort for him to talk.

"Good morning. I didn't mean to sleep all day. Someone should have woken me." Neen put a big plate of food in front of me. "Thanks. I'm sorry about your accident. What a good thing nothing's broken!" I ate, trying not to shove it all in my mouth at once. I noticed Neen was tight-lipped this morning. Maybe she was just worried about her husband.

Returning to our place was a jolt. It looked like the scene of a barroom brawl. I grabbed the straw broom and began sweeping. The tinkling glass of dishes, mementos, vases, and pictures filled the house. I stumbled over pillows and fought with feathers flying from their rips, picked up bloodstained clothes marked with dirty bootprints, and threw out curtains and shades torn from the windows. Tom broke out the rest of the glass in the bedroom window and boarded it up until we could afford some glass. How hot it was going to be without a window to open at night!

With the temperature reaching one hundred and ten degrees, we walked into the river, up to our waists. Even my fear of water was overcome by my body's need to cool off. I dipped under three times. Refreshed, I grabbed a pail and watered the wilting garden. I must keep it alive for Mother Chase. She took such pride in it. She would be home tomorrow. Tomorrow? How would we explain her husband not being here? Who would pick her up at the train? Where would she live? What would she think of me? Would I be blamed? I was full of questions but had no answers. Should I ask Tom?

I made a salad from the garden and a pot of soup at the Chases' house to keep from heating up our place. We had two bowls that weren't broken, and of course, the silverware just had to be washed. After dinner, I dared to venture, "Tom, what's going to happen when your mother gets back tomorrow?"

"Nothing," he grunted.

"Will she come here or go to Grace's?"

"Taken care of," was his reply.

"I see." Yes, I saw. I saw it wasn't any of my business, and I needed to keep my nose out of their family affairs. I liked Mother Chase. I would do my part by keeping her garden alive and see she got at least half of it. The rest was up to the Chase family—the now-silent Chase family.

The only one who would speak to me for the next month was Mother Chase.

Chapter 48

Family Visit

It was very quiet and lonely in our house by the river. Tom was gone from seven-thirty in the morning to eight-thirty at night, six days a week. What kind of a life was this? I kept myself busy with the garden, housework, and killing snakes. This was prime country for rattlesnakes; dry, hot, and rocky. I always carried a close-tined pitchfork and a heavy kitchen knife. You'd think the big rattlesnakes would be the hardest to kill, but it was actually the baby ones. They could slip out of the tines if I didn't manage to spear it. Fortunately, I was able to keep myself bite-free.

In late August, I heard a car arriving as I was weeding the garden. It was my folks in their pickup with my little sister riding in the back. "Little" was not the proper word. She was seventeen years old. I was thrilled to see them. Even though we were only six miles apart, with Tom working long hours, I had no way to visit them. I missed them and my thoughts were always wondering about them.

Papa planted eight acres into raspberries and blackcaps at their new home. The other two held the house, starts of walnut trees, apples, apricots, peaches, cherries, and a big garden. Water was plentiful in the Lewiston Orchards. That was good. Plants and trees needed lots of water in this heat. He was quite certain they'd have a good crop of berries next year. They unloaded a box of apples and a box of peaches. They looked like gold to my eyes. How I missed having fresh fruit. I grabbed a peach immediately and began to gnaw.

I pulled the kitchen chairs out to the shade on the east side of the house and got a bucket of fresh water from the river. "Sorry, you'll have to drink from the dipper. My cups and glasses got broken." I hoped they wouldn't ask questions. No one said anything.

After chitchatting, Edna wandered down to wade in the river, and Mama got up enough nerve to ask about my bruises and scrapes on my arms. "Is Tom being kind to you?" she asked, probing for the reason.

"Tom treats me well," I responded. I had never shared with them the "silent treatment." It wasn't anything they needed to know. "Oh," I suddenly realized what she was hinting about. "These bruises and scratches I got when I was exploring the empty house next door. Had some nails sticking out in unexpected places."

"I see." Mama looked doubtful, but said no more.

Edna came barefoot through the brown grass, sopping wet up to her waist. "Better watch for snakes," I called.

"What? You didn't tell me there were snakes!" she shrieked and walked slower with a close eye to the ground. She plopped herself in the chair with a squish.

"Did you tell her?" She looked from Mama to Papa. They both shook their heads. She turned her big blue eyes on me and blurted out, "I'm quitting school."

My mind cried, *Not you too. You had a chance to finish school. The chance I always wanted. The chance I was never offered because I didn't have the right shoes to go to school in town!* When I opened my mouth, I asked a simple question: "Why are you quitting?"

"'Cause everyone's mean to me. I hate the teachers. The school is too big. Besides," she glanced at the folks, "I'm in love and don't need more education. I'll marry a rich man, and he'll take care of me for the rest of my life."

I glanced at Mama and Papa. They were both looking down at their hands in their laps, not saying a word. "Edna, you are so smart. You're talented. You could get a good job someday if you finish school." I didn't know that for sure. Not many women I knew worked. There were waitresses and cooks, clerks in stores, seamstresses, and nurses. Edna turned down all those ideas.

"Nope. Don't need a job. I'm gonna marry Herman." Her lower lip came out like it used to when she was a pouty four-year-old.

"Who's Herman?" I asked, staring in disbelief. "Edna, you've only lived in Lewiston for fourteen months. You can't possibly know this man well enough to marry him." Then my memory hit me; I had only known Tom three months and six days before we got married. Who was I to tell my sister what to do? I took a deep breath. "Tell me about him."

"Well, he's twenty-three, tall and handsome with wavy blonde hair . . ."

"No, I don't want to know stuff like that. I want to know what he's like. How does he treat you? Is he a gentleman? Does he show you he loves you and wants to take care of you? Is he proud to be with you?"

"Well," she looked away. I knew she was hiding something, "He doesn't take me out in public. We just do things at our house. He works a lot so I only get to see him once or twice a week. He . . . he's . . . married." I gasped. "But, he's getting a divorce," she rapidly added.

All I could do was shake my head. "Edna, Edna, you're just asking for trouble."

"No, honest. He's getting a divorce. Then, he'll marry me."

"What will keep him from divorcing you and marrying someone else? You may be honest about this, but you can't expect a man who cheats on his wife to be honest."

She jumped to her feet and screamed at me, "You're just like them! You don't want me to be happy. I'm grown up. I can make my own decisions!" She raced to the pickup and climbed in.

I looked at Mama and Papa's sad faces and sagging shoulders. The move to the "big city" had obviously not been a good one for a teenager ready to sprout her wings. They had no control over her. I felt deep guilt for getting married and leaving my little sister. If I had stayed on the farm and continued to mother her, maybe things would have gone differently. Only God knew what was going to happen now.

Chapter 49

Escape from Isolation

After my father-in-law incident, Tom installed dead bolts on the doors and taught me how to use the shotgun—not that I thought I could ever shoot it. It was the isolation that haunted me every day. Across the river, traffic on Highway 12 was on a constant move; our side of the river had maybe three cars a week besides Tom's. I was more detached from the rest of the world than on the Stick Ranch, where people often stopped on their way to or from Reubens along with Friend and hunters. At least on the Stick Ranch, I received mail. This place didn't even have an address. There was no mail carrier all the way out here. This wasn't just the "silent wall" of Tom's withdrawing spells; this was the "silent wall" of the entire world. The only conversation day after day was with God, and it seemed so one-sided. I longed to hear people's voices in my ears.

A week before Christmas, Tom came from work to find me curled up on the bed sobbing. I had even forgotten to slip the dead bolt.

"What's going on? Father hasn't been here, has he?"

It was difficult for me to even move. The fire was low, I was cold lying on top of the covers, and it was dark. "Susie! Susie!" he yelled. "Are you all right?"

I managed a weak "yes" but inside echoed, "No . . . No, I'm not all right. I need people. I need someone to talk to. I need something productive to do. It's winter. Nothing to do. No vegetables to can, no garden to water. I can only clean this little house so many times a day. I'm sick and tired of talking to myself all day . . ." I stopped suddenly, my ears hearing my mouth verbalizing the shouts of my mind. There was silence. Oh, no! Now Tom knows how I feel and he'll put up the "silent wall" too. Sobs began again, but the tears were all cried out.

"I'm taking you to your folks. Get some clothes together. I'll come on Christmas and bring you home." He went to light the kerosene lamp and made himself a sandwich.

Guilt heaped upon guilt as I put a few items in a bag. I promised through better or worse, now I was leaving. How could I be a perfect wife and have these feelings? I should be happy just to be here with Tom. What was he going to eat while I was gone? Who was going to clean his house? Who would clean his clothes? No one would be here to greet him when he came home tired. Quietly, I climbed into the car, and he drove me to the folks.

Mama and Papa greeted us, but didn't question. "She needs her family. I'll be here Christmas for dinner and take her back with me." I heard Tom tell them. They made a makeshift bed from an old quilt on the floor in the living room. Tom had remembered my pillow. I slept hard as a rock, waking up past nine in the morning.

Edna had gone to school. They persuaded her to go one more semester. Papa was out finishing the chores. Mama was baking bread. I looked around at the familiar, well-worn furniture in the unfamiliar house. My head ached from all the tears shed last night. Guilt still played in my mind, but was quickly being replaced by a quiet peace. There were people here. People I loved as much as Tom. People who would listen to me and talk to me.

I rose and quickly trotted down the path to the outhouse. I had slept in my dress. That was convenient for my first trip of the morning. Papa was putting hay in the cow's stall as I came back. "Morning, Papa," I called.

"Morning. How'd ya sleep?" He put down his pitchfork and came to give me a hug. Papa was always the hugger. Mama, not so much. She'd put her hand on my shoulder once in a while.

"I slept so hard, I have a headache. Probably has to do with crying, too." It was cold and I began to shiver. "Can we talk? Maybe someplace warm?"

"Of course." He shut the barn door and led me to the other end where he'd built a workshop butted against the outside wall. A fire was going in the potbelly stove, and two stools sat by the bench where he'd been making a new handle for the hoe. "How do you like my new retreat?"

"Retreat?" I wanted anything but a retreat. I wanted to be with people.

"Yup. When the talk gets too much to handle in the house, I retreat out here and find something productive to do." Papa winked. "What about you? Are you retreating?"

"No . . . no, just the opposite. I need people. I miss people so much." Tears started again. Guess I stored up more during the night. I poured out my heart about the last four lonely months

"Sorry we couldn't get out to see you more." He shook his head. "It's been real important we stay here for Edna. Don't know what to do. She's so dead-burned set on this guy, on quitting school, on spoiling everything we had hopes for. She won't listen or take advice."

"I know. Papa, she's almost grown up. You can't force her."

"Doggone it. Why do kids have to grow up?" Papa looked at his hands and shook his head. "Life never turns out like you hope."

"You too, Papa? I've always wondered why I'm here. Why Mama didn't like me. Why Tom and I don't understand each other. Why Johnny took the wrong way off the farm. Why Edna doesn't appreciate all you've done for her. I wonder why I don't have any children. Is God punishing me? I feel constantly on the edge of discovering who I am but never really finding out."

We sat quietly and listened to the popping of wood in the stove. "There's a time for everything," Papa began. "There's a beginning and an end. You know from being a farm kid, there's a time to plant and a time to pick what's planted. Walking through this life, we learn when to speak up and when to keep our mouth shut. We don't want to go through those times of crying, but on the other side we laugh again. Sometimes, it seems like things are falling apart, but unless they do, we can't build something new in its place. We've got to let go of the old so we can be blessed with the new. That's the way life is. Just when ya think it's goin' well, it falls apart. But there'll come a time when you'll dance again. Keep memories of the good things and throw away the bad. Life's full of ups and downs, Susie. The only consistent thing is God. He's always there to hold us when we can't stand up, and to dance with us when we celebrate the good times. He's in charge of it all. Only he knows the beginning and the end. He makes everything beautiful in its time."

A penetrating peace floated into me. "I see what's wrong. I've been trying to make life beautiful in my time, haven't I? Thanks for your wisdom, Papa."

"Isn't my wisdom. Credit goes to a guy named Solomon thousands of years ago." Papa gave me a hug, "Now, you better get in the house before Mama thinks you froze in the outhouse." He sent me out the door with that familiar chuckle he always had.

Chapter 50

Getting Ready

My reentry into the world of people was exciting and yet alarming. Cut off from communication for many months, I heard no news, saw no newspaper, and knew nothing of what was going on in the world. The headlines of the *Tribune* on the end of the davenport startled me. "Europe Struggles." I quickly read through the article about the Depression they too were struggling with. The whole world seemed to be on hold. It was hard times for people everywhere.

Mama seemed smaller and more frail at the age of sixty-three. She hadn't been able to keep up with housekeeping during the gardening, canning, and picking season of outdoor work. I plunged in to help get ready for Christmas, chattering all the time. Mama answered my zillion questions with "Oh," "I don't know," and "I think so." I never gave her time to say much more. Another question would pop in my head as I dusted, washed doorjambs, swept and mopped floors, filled the wood box, and stirred the box of walnuts drying behind the wood heater in the living room.

By suppertime, I had run out of energy and out of words. Then I realized Edna hadn't come home from school. "Where's Edna?"

There was a "should we tell her?" look that passed between Mama and Papa. Finally, Papa said, "She's got a job after school—cooking downtown. She'll get home around eleven."

"Oh, so she's going to school and working. Well, that's good."

"She's done with school after Christmas. She refuses to go back." Mama pushed her food around the plate. "She wants to be a cook."

"She'll be a great cook." I was thinking of the wonderful pies she made when we had family get-togethers.

"S'pose so," Mama replied. I felt heavy air and decided to drop it. After a bit Mama muttered, "Just wish she'd practice some 'round here."

I breathed deep and quickly changed the subject. "Where do you want to put the Christmas tree?"

"We've had it in that far corner of the living room by the davenport." Papa pointed. "I'll get my things cleared out so there'll be room."

I quickly cleared the table and washed the dishes. Mama dried. "What will we cook for Christmas dinner?" I asked.

"There's a ham in the root cellar I've been saving."

"I'll make potato salad and baked beans. Maybe Edna will make a pie." I could taste it all now. We'd been living on vegetables, soups, and whatever I could make from the milk Tom brought home from work: cottage cheese, pudding, brick cheese . . . It would be a treat to have a regular meal. Mama seemed relieved to have help.

School was out for Christmas break the next day. I helped Edna dig out the tree decorations, and of course, the fuzzy, old, red and white wreath with one electric candle in the center that was always placed in a window. We laughed and talked about them. Many of them were handmade—wooden or cardboard painted by us kids. Some were store-bought last year—their first year in the big city. "Which one has the most memories for you?" I asked my sister.

"This one." She held up a hand-drawn, painted nativity from our last year together before I got married. "It's the last thing you made with me. You always took time to do things with me. You loved me."

"Oh, honey. I still do. You'll always be my little girl. I got to take care of you from the time you were a baby till I left home. I'll love you forever." There were tears in both our eyes as we hugged for a long time. "I want the very best for you. Are you sure you're making good decisions?" She nodded. "I hope so." My heart was crying for her future.

The next day, Papa brought home a little tree. Edna and I carefully strung the new set of electric Christmas lights. The round, red and green bulbs were about half the size of a regular light bulb. We thought they were just the "cat's meow." We made a game of saying something nice about each decoration as we strategically placed it. Coming to the last one, which Johnny had made, we were without words. We carefully placed it front and center. His presence with us. Mama would shed silent tears when she saw it, but we couldn't leave it off. For all the teasing and meanness he dealt out as we were growing up, he was still a part of us and we wished he were here.

We were ready for Christmas.

Chapter 51

Happy Christmas to All

Christmas Day, 1935! I got up early to stoke the wood in the cookstove that I had polished the day before. It gleamed black with sparkling silver trim ready to help us celebrate. I mixed beans in the brown, two-handled bean pot and put in my secret ingredient along with pieces of bacon and apples. The potatoes and eggs were boiled, and the ham was stuck in the oven to keep the beans company. The secret to keeping it all just the right temperature was how much and what kind of wood was put in the firebox and where each item was placed on the stove. The oven had to be slow cooking; the lids above the firebox had to be hot enough to boil water.

Mama mixed up a batch of her unbelievable rolls and set them to rise in the warmer oven above the cooking area. I would have been happy with just those for dinner. Mine never tasted the same. Edna had made pies the day before: cherry and apple. The smells were driving my stomach crazy. Ah, now just to wait.

Tom arrived around ten with his arms loaded with packages. My husband had gone Christmas shopping? I didn't know he could do that. They were even wrapped. He gently set them on the floor and went back for more. My goodness, where did this all come from? Added to what the folks had under the tree, it looked like St. Nicholas remembered we'd been good boys and girls.

Mama and Papa had taken my wind-up phonograph to their house for safekeeping when we found out we had to move from the Stick

Ranch and weren't settled. I dug through the stack in its cabinet and found a Christmas album. We put the record on and sang along to the familiar carols. Edna and I competed in who could sing the loudest until Mama said, "Hush it down!" I read "A Visit from St. Nicholas" just like I did every year to my sister. Laughing, visiting, sharing memories—all was healing to my soul.

We were startled by the telephone ringing on the wall—two long and one short, the folks' ring.

Mama reached up and removed the black receiver from the wooden box. "Hello." There was a pause. She turned white. I quickly put a chair for her to sit, but the telephone was too high. She shook her head and stood bravely. "It's Johnny. He says, 'Merry Christmas' to everyone." "Merry Christmas to you too, son."

Papa hightailed it from the living room, putting his ear down to the receiver to listen with Mama. "Merry Christmas, Johnny," he spoke loudly into the belled piece. "We miss you." That's all he could say as his voice cracked.

"Thanks for calling." Mama was in tears. "I know this is costing a lot of money, so I'll say goodbye. Yes, yes, you too." She plopped into the chair and wept. The only sounds in the house were falling tears and happy sobs. Handkerchiefs were pulled out of pockets, eyes wiped, and noses blown. Each lost in our own thoughts. Our brother and son had come home for a few Christmas minutes—the first we'd heard from him in eighteen months.

Dinner seemed unimportant after the gift of the phone call. Holiday meals were always eaten around three in the afternoon and were called dinner instead of supper. We ate until we could hold no more, washed the dishes, and then ate some more in the evening. Food was never taken off the table, so it was a process of nibbling our way through the day.

Today, being Christmas, there was the distraction of opening presents after the dishes were washed. We sat in a circle in the living room, and Edna, being the youngest, got to pass out the gifts. No one opened until the packages were to their rightful owners. Then sister got to choose which of hers she'd open first. She chose the one from Papa and Mama. It was a big, heavy box, scooted not lifted. Inside? Her own set of cast ironware. "If you're gonna be a cook, you've got to have the right pans." Papa winked. It was their way of letting her know they accepted her choice. She hugged Papa and took Mama's hand and said, "Thank you. Thanks for understanding."

Mama gave us a set of everyday dishes collected from flour sacks. Golden Mill Flour Company put a different dish in each flour sack as a buying incentive. They were perfect. Plain, white, sturdy, and much needed at our house. We had a pink glass setting for eight at the folks, a wedding present that we didn't want to claim until we had permanent housing; someday, I hoped. Papa had built Tom a tool cabinet with a place for everything. Edna had made a tin of cookies at work. Mmmm. We'd save those until later.

Now, what did Tom bring? A seat cover for Papa's pickup, a warm housecoat for Mama, a sweater for Edna, and for me? A radio and five books! I couldn't have been more thrilled. Something to listen to, something to do during the long, lonely days. My husband had done well. Plus, he brought old-fashioned chocolates for everyone, including himself. He was grinning ear to ear. My heart was so happy. In one week, I had gone from being in the dumps up to the mountaintop.

Before we left for home, Papa pulled out his well-worn Bible and read the Christmas story. That's what today was all about: Love—a loving God giving us the gift of His Son, showing us how to love each other. For one day, I felt all was right with the world and I could say, "Happy Christmas to all, and to all a good night."

Chapter 52

A Bridge

New Year's. I couldn't face Tom's father. The traditional Chase dinner was going to be at Neen's. All the family would be there. My fear hovered too near the surface to be exposed. I would feel his angry, lurking eyes following me. Tom understood. I fixed a potato salad and baked beans for him to share.

He dropped me off at the folks for the day. No one asked about me except Mother Chase. We kept the "incident" a secret from her. "She's not feeling well," was Tom's excuse we had decided on.

"Oh, is she with child?" was her comeback, he told me. Tom had shaken his head no immediately, feeling guilt for not producing Chase offspring.

When he picked me up, we rode silently home. I knew a wall had formed in my absence. I must be patient. I must be loving. I must . . . Why did I fall right back into the fix-it pattern? What did Papa say? "He makes all things beautiful in His time."

After a week, life returned to normal routine. The radio was great company. I found a station that had wonderful continued stories. Later, I learned they were called soap operas. What a strange name. They got their name by being sponsored by companies who sold cleaning products. They were a radio drama series about typical daily events in the lives of the same group of characters. The Smith Family was the first I found. Then I discovered Fibber McGee and Molly. Oh, my, how I would laugh—especially at his closet that was so stuffed, they didn't dare open the door. They were so silly. My grandmama was right, laughter is good medicine. I found myself feeling better and better, singing along and dancing to the music. It was the best gift Tom could have given me.

In April of 1936, Tom came home early in the day. "Are you all right?" I questioned. He would never leave work unless he was dying. "Here, sit down. Can I get you a glass of water? Coffee? Bread?" I found myself in a panic. What could be wrong?

"Whoa! Slow down. Sit. I have something to tell you." He pointed to a chair. I shut my mouth and sat ready for the next disaster in our life. "Charlie gave me the day off. He said, 'Tom, you need to get a better job than scooping cow pies and milking all day. I hear the Camas Prairie Railroad's hiring, now that the economy's picking up. You get yourself down there and apply for a job. Railroading is good, decent work and pays pretty well.' So, I went down today, filled out an application, and talked to the boss. He hired me on the spot. I'm gonna be fixin' up railcars in the roundhouse."

"What? Is this true? I'm gonna be married to a rail-driving man?" I had two uncles on Mama's side that worked for the railroad most of their lives. Aunt Phoebe owned a hotel in Reubens that catered to railroaders who stayed overnight before heading back to Lewiston. Now, my man was going to be one of them. I jumped up, grabbed Tom, and danced him around the kitchen singing, "I've been working on the railroad, all the live long day. . ."

Out of breath, we both fell into chairs laughing. After the hard times of the last eight years, I saw a light at the end of the tunnel . . . a train tunnel!

Tom stood and took my hands and said, "I have to go up to the ranch and tell Charlie I won't be coming to work tomorrow. They want me to start in the morning."

He gave me a hug and a kiss, and headed out to say goodbye to the cow-tending business. How great it would be not to have the house smelling like manure all the time. Even though he left his tall rubber boots outside the door after he washed them off in the river, his clothes carried that odor wherever he went.

Charlie was right. The railroad paid almost twice what Tom was getting on the dairy ranch. Bless his heart for the suggestion. The Kerbys were good folks. Always looking out for others' well-being, even though it might mean harder times for themselves.

Tom had a lot of learning to do. Russell was a good teacher. He'd been in the roundhouse for twenty years. Knew it all. Tom caught on quick when it came to doing things with his hands. He was able to be on his own, repairing railcar beds after just a month. They were pleased with his work.

As an added bonus, he worked the swing shift from three in the afternoon to eleven at night. In those winter mornings, I read to Tom the books he'd given me for Christmas. The saleslady in the store had picked out some classics. I started with *Moby Dick*. Tom was mesmerized. With only a third grade education, he never heard the wonderful adventures found in books.

Another bonus was two days off. Since he was the new guy at work, he didn't get two days together or his choice of days, but he did have two full days. We spent one day going to Lewiston, shopping and visiting either his family or mine. What a treat that was for me. The second day, we worked on repairs around the house. The bedroom window still hadn't been replaced, and the house needed calcimine inside. We were still the only occupied house, so we needed to keep the brush down around the other houses. We didn't want the owners raising our five-dollar-a-month rent.

It was out with the cow smell and in with the grease—ugh! Not ordinary grease but thick, smelly grease. After two days of wear, the coveralls could stand up in the corner all by themselves. Tom only had two pairs. The washboard and tub sat in the middle of the kitchen while I boiled water daily with shaved bars of homemade lye soap. In would go the coveralls, boiled for fifteen minutes, transferred into the washtub with a big stick, then hand-scrubbed on the board; back into the boiling water, repeating this for three rounds. The sun dried them in about three hours on the clothesline. My hands were raw. On the first payday, we bought two more pairs of coveralls, Bag Balm, and rubber gloves.

When I was mindlessly scrubbing one day, my thoughts wandered to life—my life. *It's like a bridge. I span from my pioneer parents' covered wagon and immigrant train days, to travel by car with airplanes flying overhead. I've lived in isolation and transitioned to easy communication by radio and telephone. I look forward to embracing new inventions to make life easier. I bridge between the folks and Edna, Tom and his family, even Tom and books. What about the next generation? When was I ever going to produce a child who would be the bridge to our family's future?*

Chapter 53

Sibling Heartaches

It was easy being frugal in our isolation of the past year. Now, we were tempted every time we went to town. More than anything, we wanted to save enough to buy our own place. We put away ten dollars out of Tom's forty-dollar paycheck every month. One of our stops in town was always the bank. At first, we shied away from having anything to do with the banks because of the Depression, but the First Bank of Idaho assured us our money was safe because it was insured by the government. It didn't dawn on us that the government might have money problems too. We opened a savings account and rented a safety deposit box to keep our "important papers" in—paystubs, marriage license, and our savings passbook.

The berry crop was coming on. I asked, "Can you drop me at the folks on your way to town today? I want to help them pick. They're coming on fast."

"Tell you what. Let's stop at the bank then we'll both help." Tom parked in front of the bank and dashed in to do our banking. I giggled with delight at the thought of having banking business. I stayed in the car, away from shopping temptations.

It took all day for four of us to pick the raspberry patch clean. Papa had used lots of fertilizer and water, and they were beautiful big berries.

At the end of the day, Tom and Papa climbed into the pickup and took them to the grocery store in Lewiston. The owner bought them for one dollar a flat. Each flat held twelve *halics*. That was Papa's Dutch word for berry basket. The grocer sold them to customers for ten cents each *halic*, making a twenty-cent profit. Papa came home with fifteen dollars. Not bad for the first picking.

"Sure helped having you pick. Could use your help again, Susie," Papa commented. We struck a deal. I'd stay at the folks and help pick on the days Tom worked.

We got an early start each day. Even with taking time out for lunch, we were done by the time it got hot. Edna was off cooking early, so they couldn't count on her help. I'd pick as much as I could, but it looked like they'd need to hire help.

After three weeks of raspberries, the blackcaps came on. They were my favorite to pick. They looked like a raspberry, but were black and firm with a unique flavor. They added up quickly in the halic. Because they were rare, they brought a higher price at the store.

I thought Mama and Papa had a good start on their new little farm. I have to admit, I was glad when berry season was over and I could spend more time with Tom.

We were on the last picking of the season when an unknown but familiar car drove in. All our heads popped up out of the bushes. We couldn't believe our eyes when we saw Johnny walking toward us. "Had a hard time finding your place," he grinned. "Had to finally ask at the grocery store.

"Johnny!" "Johnny?" "Johnny!" We all cried. "Why didn't you let us know you were coming?"

He shuffled his feet and looked away. "We've been here for seven months."

"What? I don't understand." Mama was wide eyed. "You've been living here for seven months and didn't come see us?"

Papa and I looked at each other. We knew why. "Is Alice with you?" Papa asked quietly.

"No. She's at the house." Johnny's face was full of emotions—shame, anger, hurt. "I needed to come alone. I . . . I need to know . . . am I still your son?"

Mama's piercing blue eyes drilled him for a moment in anger, then softened. "Of course, son . . ." After a long pause, Mama said, "But Alice will never be my daughter."

Johnny was working at the mill and Alice in a grocery store. It seems California hadn't been the pot of gold at the end of the rainbow.

They lived with Uncle Martin a short time. He got tired of Alice's complaining and nagging. They moved to a migrant worker's one-room shack in the orange orchard and worked as hired hands. Life wasn't rosy. They were back, eating crow—especially Alice.

Neither Papa nor I said anything about the money they took. Mama had never been told. It was time to move on.

Our routine became comfortable and life seemed good. Summer tumbled into fall, and fall fell into winter. It was snowing at our river house by the first of December.

Along with the snow came a visitor one morning. I didn't recognize the car, but knew the passenger—Edna. I went out the door to greet her and glanced at the driver, a suave-looking man with wavy blonde hair. "We've gotta talk," she commanded as she took me by the elbow and steered me into the house. Inside, the hard-crusted attitude melted as she folded onto the settee and burst into tears. I took her into my arms.

"Edna, Edna, talk to me. What's going on?" Attempting to speak through the sobs, I couldn't understand a word. "Go ahead. Cry your heart out. Then you can explain to me."

Finally getting control, she confessed, "You were right, Susie. He's nothing but trouble. He's not going to leave his wife or get a divorce. He says he can't because it would ruin his kids' lives."

"Is that him in the car?" She nodded. I glanced out the window. "Should I invite him in?" She shook her head.

"He says he loves me, but I can't believe him . . ." Tears washed my little sister's face. "He won't even leave her now that . . . I'm . . . I'm going to have his baby. Susie, I'm pregnant!"

This couldn't be happening! Not to my little sister. Oh, God, what now? What do I do

now?

"Have you told the folks?" I knew how this would tear Papa apart. I felt this news bending me so low, I couldn't stand up.

Edna shook her head. "I wanted to tell you first. You were the one who cared for me, loved me, taught me. Mama never loved me. I heard her say to Papa one day, 'You take care of her problem, John. You were the one who wanted another child.' She's just put up with me. I just want to be loved."

I rubbed her back, "I love you, Edna."

"Yes," she looked at me with swollen, red eyes. "Yes, I know you do. But you left me to marry Tom. You found someone else to love you." I felt suffocating guilt heaped on me. "I want someone else to love me, too."

It became so quiet, I could hear the wind-up alarm clock ticking in the bedroom. I had no argument. I had put my own need to escape in front of the little girl I had raised. That was in the past. This was now, and there had to be some kind of future plan.

I was finally able to stand. "I'll go with you to tell the folks. They need to be part of the plan. When's your next day off work?"

"Friday," she sniffled. "I haven't told them at work yet. I know I'll lose my job. They can't have an unwed pregnant woman working as their cook. It would ruin their reputation."

Edna had cried her way through several of my handkerchiefs. She dabbed her eyes one last time. "I'll have Tom drop me off when he goes to town," I promised. "We'll tell them together."

She nodded, and I walked her out to the car. I nodded to Herman. He nodded back. What else should I have done in this first meeting? I felt resentment, furious that he had led Edna on. What was he going to do to make this right? It sounded like nothing. They drove away in the gathering darkness.

Back in the privacy of our house, I shouted to God, "How could you let this happen? It should be me that's pregnant! Why isn't it me?"

Chapter 54

An Advocate

Fear thundered through my emotions. It rumbled and crashed from mind to heart in an overpowering storm. I can't tell Tom about Edna. His reaction will be the same as mine—ranting at God, but I would get the brunt of it. I lay awake when he got home from work, but pretended sleep. My words were not yet formulated to explain the calamity exploding in my life.

Tom got up first in the morning. He started the fire in the kitchen stove, a habit left over from our winters on the Stick Ranch. He set the coffee pot on to boil. I was exhausted from lack of sleep. He slammed the outside door. I knew I couldn't put this off. I crawled out of bed and dressed quickly in the still-cold house. He swept the new fallen snow off the steps and made a path out to the car. The coffee smelled good. It always smelled good, like it was announcing a new day, a new start. I never developed a taste for it, but it wouldn't be morning without the smell of coffee. I made oatmeal and mixed up the pancake batter. "Wish I had some eggs," I said to myself.

"You're quiet this mornin'," Tom commented as he watched me move around the kitchen. "Somethin' wrong?"

Funny, I thought. Tom could be quiet for weeks. It hasn't been an hour and he's asking why I'm quiet.

I took a deep breath as I put breakfast on the table and sat down. "I had a visitor yesterday." Tom's head jerked back from his fork. "No, it wasn't your father. It was Edna."

"Oh?" Tom poured his coffee into his saucer to cool and sat his cup on the table. "And?"

"She came to share some news with me."

"Good news or bad news? The folks okay?" Tom was ignoring the food and staring at me. "Uh, she's . . . she's . . . she's going to have a baby." I just blurted it out. All the well-thought-out words had deserted my mind.

"What?" Tom yelled, jumping up from the table, nearly tipping it over. Coffee spilled everywhere. "What are you talking about, woman? She can't have a baby. It's not s'pose to happen like this. She's not married and she's gonna have a baby? We've been married eight years and haven't had even one pregnancy. It's not s'pose to happen like this!"

Tom was yelling at me. Where was the silent treatment? Where's the retreating into your shell, Tom? Just when I thought I knew what to expect, life took another turn. I sat and waited, wordless, because my heart was chanting along with him.

When he ran out of steam, he sat down, took a sip of what was left of his coffee, refilled his saucer, and looked at me. "What did she want ya to do about it?"

"She wanted me to know first. We're going to tell the folks on Friday. We'll make a plan together. We still need to love her, Tom. It's not her fault we don't have a baby."

"How'd she get all the way out here? Walk?" Tom ate slowly.

"No, he brought her in his car." I had to be honest even knowing that Tom would be angry.

"He was here—in this house? Good thing I wasn't here or you'd be visiting me in jail."

"He stayed in the car. I was glad. I don't know what I would have said to him. He refuses to get a divorce. It won't be good for his kids. Now he's going to have another one and you wanna bet he won't claim it?" I shook my head and sighed. "I don't know what Edna's going to do. She'll lose her job. Papa doesn't have money to pay for a doctor, let alone at the age of fifty-six and Mama being sixty-four, raising another child? How will Mama stand having a baby in the house at that age? She didn't even like babies when I was born." I was trying to think things through out loud. "I don't know. I just don't know."

Tom was quiet for a long time. "Maybe we should raise the baby."

I shook my head. "I'm not sure Edna would let that happen. I'll suggest it. Thanks. That thought hadn't even occurred to me."

The next two days dragged by. I wracked my brain for answers to this dilemma. I made a list of possibilities. Tom's suggestion kept floating to the top. Is this how I'm supposed to have a child? I questioned over and over.

Tom dropped me off and went to town alone to do banking, shopping, and visiting. A trip to town always entailed seeing friends and stopping to "chew the fat" for an hour or so. That would give us plenty of time alone with the folks.

After some chitchat, I said, "Mama, Papa, come sit in the living room. Edna and I have something we'd like to share with you." I was boldly directing the scene on the outside, but quaking on the inside. With Papa in his brown leather chair and Mama in her little rocking chair, Edna and I sat on the davenport. I put the pillow in my lap and hung on for dear life. Edna twisted the daylights out of a hanky in her hands. How was this going to be received? "Edna has some news that could be good news or could be bad news."

Edna took a deep breath and simply said, "Mama, Papa . . . I'm going to have a baby."

Mama and Papa looked at each other and nodded. Mama responded, "Yes, I already knew that."

"How could you know? I've only told Herman and Susie," Edna cried.

"A mother has ways of knowing without words, daughter. I've known a while."

Papa asked the all-important question, "What are your plans?"

Edna twisted the hanky. "I don't have any. Herman's promised to pay for the doctor and the hospital if I won't tell them who the father is. He doesn't want anything more to do with me or the baby."

It was my turn to be surprised. "Really? That's good. He does have one decent spot left in his heart," I said bitterly.

Edna looked at me with tears. "This is as much my fault as his. I've got to take the
responsibility of raising this baby."

With that statement, I decided not to even suggest Tom and I could raise this child. It wouldn't be easy, but it was going to help Edna grow up—quickly.

"When's the baby due?" Mama asked with wet blue eyes.

There was deep relief on Edna's strained face. "The doctor says sometime in May. Herman took me to see him a few weeks ago."

"Your mother and I've already talked about this. You'll stay here as long as it takes you to get on your feet enough to support yourself and the baby." Papa gave a sad smile. "We're sorry it turned out this way. We want you to know we still love you." Wowzie! I never could have imagined what was happening before my eyes. Edna was going to be all right.

When Tom came, he brought his favorite old-fashioned chocolates to share with everyone. It was a small celebration. Mama and Papa were at last going to be grandparents, and I was going to be an aunt—just one step down from being a mother.

Tom and I rode home with some comfort that all would be well in the Kole household. We, more than ever, had no contentment. We longed for the joy a child could bring to the Chase household.

Chapter 55

House Hunting

The second week of December, Tom declared, "I think we've got enough saved to go lookin' for a place to buy. I heard there's property in the Orchards that's gone in default because of unpaid taxes and irrigation district dues. We can probably get it for a good price."

"You really think that's possible? What does default mean?" I questioned. We only had a hundred and forty-two dollars in the savings. It was a huge amount to us. The most we ever saved. It should have been more. We took out some to fix the car, get work overalls and boots for Tom's new job, and repair the damage his father had caused.

"When someone doesn't pay what's owed in taxes, water, or the mortgage, it goes back to whoever owned it before—the city, mortgage company or the irrigation district. How 'bout taking a drive up there tomorrow before I go to work?" Tom grinned. I could tell he was excited.

His hazel eyes sparkled.

I was too, but there was also this nagging fear that it was just another move. We had moved five times in our eight years of marriage: four times the first year, spent five years on the Stick Ranch, and now two years of isolation on the river. I wanted so badly to be permanently settled. This dream was second only to having a baby.

It took forty-five minutes to reach the property on Grelle between Twentieth and Twenty-First streets. Ten acres of flat, usable land lay to the north. A two-room shack sat at the end of a long, muddy driveway.

The black tar paper roof looked new, but it had no permanent roofing. A new material called fake brick asbestos had been rolled around the outside walls, attempting to make it attractive.

A wood cookstove stood against the entry wall of the kitchen. A tall, red water pump was piped into the opposite corner. One small window slid up from the bottom. The front and backdoors created a straight path through the fifteen-by-fifteen-foot kitchen. The other room would serve as a combination of living room and bedroom. It also had a small slide-up window, but no outside door. An archway connected the two rooms All totaled, there was around 400 square feet. The outhouse stood a good fifty feet from the kitchen backdoor. That was the sum total of buildings. A bonus was the fruit trees: apple, peach, and prune. Otherwise, long grass and untilled ground covered the entire acreage. It looked like a lot of work to me.

We leaned against the front of the car and stared for a long time, each trying to imagine what it could look like ten years from now. "Thoughts?" asked Tom.

"Every bit of it could be planted." I was trying hard to be positive.

"It's not big enough to make a living off. I'd still have to work." Tom stated it matter-of-factly, like it was just going to be that way. It didn't make any difference to him.

I said a silent thank-you. I was tired of struggling to live off the land. My heart yearned to be in a secure, fruitful place. The Lord hadn't let us starve, but he'd certainly taught us how to earn our keep by hard labor. "We could plant more fruit trees all the way out to the road. I've missed fresh fruit and canning for winter. A pear tree and an apricot would be perfect," I added.

Tom pointed, "I could see putting a barn back there to the left of the outhouse. It would need to be tall enough for a hayloft. There could be a pasture around it. All this over here, we could plant to alfalfa. Cows do well on it." We were catching a picture of what it could be. "I've got tomorrow off. Let's go talk to the county clerk." We rode home, wrapped in dreams.

We were two greenhorn kids who had no idea what the buying process was. Mary Gilmore, the Nez Perce County treasurer, was very kind, taking time to explain. "The back taxes and water rights have to be paid in cash. That amounts to one hundred and fifty-one dollars and ninety-six cents. Then you can apply for a mortgage to buy the land for the asking price of three hundred and seventy-five dollars."

I'm sure she noticed our quick exchange of disbelief. "How hard is it to get a mortgage?" Tom inquired. He hadn't even worked for the railroad a year. Would they trust us?

"Are you regularly employed?" she questioned.

"Uh, I guess you'd call it that. I've worked for the railroad since April. They tell me I'm a good worker and they want ta keep me on."

"Good, good. Do you have enough cash to pay the back money owed?" she asked, smiling at us with friendly blue eyes.

I found my proud voice responding, "Oh yes. We've been saving every payday since he got hired at the railroad." However, my mind was questioning: where we would get the extra ten dollars.

"Then don't worry. I'm sure they'll accept you. First, I want you to take these home and fill them out as accurately as possible." She shoved a stack of papers toward us. "Then this," she handed me a roll of papers bound by yellow oilcloth. "This is called the 'Abstract of Title' to the property. An abstract is the history of the piece of property. Read it carefully. Make sure you know there are no more liens against the land so you won't be charged extra. Bring everything back to me by next Tuesday and we'll get you started on your mortgage."

We walked back to the car, stunned by how fast all that had transpired. We hadn't signed anything yet so we weren't panicked. Three hundred and seventy-five dollars! That's a lot of money. We counted on our one hundred forty-two dollars being a cushion to help during tight times. Would this be possible?

I read the loan papers out loud. The terms were confusing. We would secure a "promissory note for purchasing Lot 6, Block 92, Lewiston Orchards for $375, due on or before December 1 of 1941, with interest on all deferred payments at the rate of 6% per annum from the date hereof, interest payable annually." This included the real property and "water rights or shares of stock or water of any ditch or irrigation company situated in Nez Perce County, Idaho."

We hadn't realized how much power the irrigation company held. We saw the fancy office they built after the folks bought the old water office building. So this is where they were getting their money—from the property owners.

We began adding up the figures: $75 a year on the principle, approximately $22 for interest on the loan, and $148 for taxes and water . . . my goodness, that was $243 a year! Tom's yearly take home pay was $480. Could we possibly live on $235 a year? This needed time to think—and pray.

Chapter 56

Looking Back, Looking Forward

Tom went to work the next day. I started reading the oilcloth-bound abstract. My goodness, what a history that piece of property has. The first page was a certified copy of the United States patent in 1884 given to William Eakin, one hundred acres for the sum of two hundred dollars. It was signed by President Grover Cleveland. Mr. Eakin sold it to Donald Davidson and Patrick Campbell in 1887 for eight hundred dollars at 12 percent interest, and they in turn sold eighty acres to Mrs. C. L. Stevens for three hundred and fifty dollars in 1888. Then, it seems everyone defaulted on their payments and the land reverted back to the mortgage company in Salem, Oregon, which was owned by a company in Great Britain and Scotland with its main office in Dublin, Ireland. Who did this property belong to in the first place? Did President Cleveland have the right to sell it?

After it had changed hands several times, with interest sometimes as high as 18 percent, Charles L. Gifford purchased the same one hundred sixty acres plus four hundred and eighty more, paying three thousand five hundred dollars in cash. The mortgage company wasn't going to let go so easily and filed a quick claim deed through the Salem Bank, which was now owned by a company in Amsterdam, Netherlands. It was an international problem. In 1910, an Idaho judge awarded the property free and clear to the Giffords, severing all international ties. Mr. Gifford was a smart business man. He sold it off by lots and blocks. Lot 6 at 2023 Grelle sold for two thousand two hundred and sixty-five dollars that year. Again it was sold in 1924, along with other land, to John and Mabel Wilks for one thousand five hundred dollars, but they couldn't pay the taxes and it defaulted to Nez Perce County. Now, they were offering it to us for three hundred seventy-five dollars. The Depression had been kind to us in the long run.

Could we make the payments? Or would we join the long line of owners who had defaulted? It would be tight. We'd been living on a shoestring ever since we got married. What's five more years? We could survive, but would we thrive?

I carefully filled out all the paperwork Mrs. Gilmore gave us. Then I started figuring how we'd live on what was left.

The next morning, I had everything ready to show my husband. After breakfast, I proudly placed it all before him—the neatly printed paperwork, the solution of where the extra ten dollars was going to come from, and the month-by-month budget that would help us save enough every year to make the mortgage payments plus pay the taxes and water. We wouldn't be able to have electricity or phone, but we could live without that. We'd limit our trips, plan our visits to the folks and Neens either on the way to do town business or on the way back. Gas would be the greatest need on the list so Tom could get to his work. A gallon a week would do it, and at ten cents a gallon, we could figure forty cents a month.

I would can fruit without sugar and vegetables without salt. I'd bake all of our bread. We needed to buy a cow and some chickens right away so we'd have milk and eggs. That meant building a fence, a barn, and a pen. No trees grew around here. We'd have to buy posts and wire. That would be our big expense the first year. We could cut the grass for hay the first few years till we could afford the alfalfa seeds.

"See," I said when he looked up at me. "We can do it."

Tom looked at me with a twinkle in his eye. "What did I ever do to deserve you?" I felt warm, loved, and accepted by my handsome man. I'd done my part to bridge between nomadic life and a permanent home.

On Tom's next day off, we went to the clerk's office with papers in hand. Mrs. Gilmore looked them over. "I'll get these filed right away. That will be one dollar for the filing."

Tom walked the block to the bank to draw out one dollar. Were there going to be other hidden costs she hadn't told us about? We decided not to tell anyone about our plans, just in case things fell through. This was a giant, scary step in Mr. and Mrs. Tom Chase's life. It turned out to be the best decision we ever made.

We left the courthouse giddy as school girls. I did some light Christmas shopping. Tom bought his usual old-fashioned chocolates to share with everyone at Christmas Day. Couldn't spend much this year since we just pledged to empty our entire savings account.

As we were walking to our car, we ran into the folks. Papa invited us. "Come, have a donut à la mode with us. I'll buy." And then he led the way to the donut shop on Main Street. It was my favorite treat in town—a warm, plain, crispy donut with a large scoop of vanilla ice cream on top. Little did he know this was our secret celebration. We were going to be homeowners.

Chapter 57

We Did It!

After Christmas, Edna quit her job and found a position taking care of children in the home of a wealthy family. It didn't pay much, but they picked her up and brought her home. She ate lunch with the three kids. Sometimes, she fixed dinner for them when the parents were out to some event. The mother didn't work, but was involved in volunteer work and high-society goings-on in the city of Lewiston. She didn't seem to mind Edna's situation.

We gave notice to the landlord December 1 and moved most of our meager possessions out of the river house right after Christmas. We didn't have to pay January's rent, and by adding some of our grocery money, we made up the ten dollars for the cash payment. On December 31, 1936, we signed the final papers for our new home. New Year's Eve, we slept in our own bed, in our own house!

We even brought our woodpile with us, which we gleaned from the mill in Spaulding. Mill ends and bark were good for the taking at most mills; kept us warm most winters. "I'll get a fire going to warm up the house before night," Tom said, as he put wood in the kitchen stove and lit the kindling. Immediately, the house filled with smoke. We doused the fire and opened windows and doors. A bird had built its nest in the flue. Tom had to take the chimney apart and clean it out. Good thing he did. There was soot build-up inside that could have caught fire. Nothing'sscarier than the roar of a chimney fire with flames shooting out the top—especially with nothing but a tar paper roof.

We told the folks and Edna on Christmas Day. Our news was greeted by smiles, laughter, and congratulations. No one cared about the small gifts we gave. They were thrilled we would finally be settled in a place of our own.

Before New Year's Day, Tom warned his sister that we couldn't bring anything to share for dinner. We were moving. We wouldn't give them an exact address to keep it a secret from his father. Tom's father didn't come. He wasn't feeling well. I breathed a prayer of thanks and then felt guilty for wishing him ill. Grace and Jim had brought Mother Chase.

It was a full house. All of Tom's family was there except Frankie who lived in Portland. The living room seemed very small. Adults sat in chairs; kids sat on the floor.

"So." Neen looked around the crowd. "I think Tom and Susie have something important to tell us."

Immediately, Mother Chase yelled out, "You're gonna have a baby?" She wanted us to have a child as much as we did.

Everyone was very quiet as Tom and I shook our heads. "Nope," Tom looked around and grinned. "We just bought us a place." Everyone began talking at once. Questions were answered with caution so as not to reveal the location. My husband stood proud among his family that day.

Home Sweet Susan Chase
Home

The next week at work, Everett Leachman, who had been at the mill, started working for the railroad. Everett was married to my cousin, Lucy. It turned out they lived on the corner of Grelle and Lindsey Creek, just an eighth of a mile from us. A block in the Lewiston Orchards at that time was a quarter of a mile long. It took four blocks to make a mile. Each block was broken into ten-acre lots. The Leachmans were already pretty well set-up with a house and barn. They had a family of three kids.

"What are yer plans for the property?" Everett asked one day at work during supper break.

"Got ta build a barn and fence a pasture, and make a chicken coop so we can get some critters. Don't know where we'll get the money for all that. It'll work out somehow." Tom stuffed the last of his bread and bacon grease sandwich into his mouth.

"Can I tell ya a secret?" Everett said as he moved closer to Tom. "I was just working at the mill, ya know. They put all the cull boards in a pile out near the road. You can have them just for the hauling."

"What? You're kidding." Tom's unbelief sometimes rivaled his namesake.

"Nope. When our shift's over tonight, follow me and we'll load up some for your place."

So began the great lumber express. Every night, Tom and Everett would go by the cull drop and pick up all they could haul. Sometimes, there'd only be a board or two, and sometimes there'd be so many, they couldn't get them all in their cars. The stack of lumber at the end of our humble home grew taller and wider than the house itself, as the winter began to let go and the weather warmed. It would make a fine barn and coop.

Tom began going to work early to collect big rocks along the riverside of the railroad yard. Sometimes, bent rails that couldn't be straightened were free if you could load them. By April, we dug ditches and laid rocks and rails as the foundation for the barn and coop. Old memories came flooding back of rock-hard trenches dug for the log cabin. This was easy in comparison. By the middle of May, we had a barn that any cow would be proud to live in, and it hadn't cost a cent—except for the nails.

We needed a fence, but fence posts would have to wait till after Edna's baby was born. Papa needed his vehicle close at hand to make the run to the hospital. Papa's pickup would take us to Waha Mountain to cut trees and make posts. We were experts at that.

Herman was true to his word, paying cash for all the baby's bills. Patricia Joy was born at White Hospital in Lewiston on May 22, 1937. She was the first in our family to be born in a hospital. She was a beautiful, blond-haired baby with big, blue eyes. I loved her at first sight, but found I couldn't completely shove the jealousy out of my heart.

Shortly afterward, Herman was drafted into the army.

Chapter 58

A Cow of Our Own

On Tom's days off, we drove to Waha Mountain in Papa's old pickup to cut down trees and saw them into fence posts before berries set on at the folks. We stripped the bark and dipped the bottom three feet in leftover tar we got from the road crew when they finished paving Grelle. We buried them five feet apart then nailed two cull boards diagonally from the top of one post to the bottom of the next, making an X on the inside so the cow couldn't push the fence apart. The fence took longer to build than the barn. It was a good enclosure with plenty of green grass.

We were ready for our cow. This presented several problems. We had no idea how much cows were going for. The auction only happens on Saturdays. Tom works that day. Women never attended auctions. Also, how in the world would we get a cow from the sales yard down by the railroad, to our house? It was about ten miles. Too far to lead her.

Tom talked it over with Papa. "Well," he answered. "We usually got a new milk cow from some neighbor when we lived in Reubens. Just led it home behind the horse. Guess you can't do that here though with all the traffic. Now Bossie, we got from the Martins next door when she was just a young heifer. Think we paid ten dollars for her. I've got racks for the pickup, you know. You could haul an animal back there." There was a solution to one problem. Ten dollars? That was a lot. Maybe we couldn't get a cow right away.

We turned our attention to the chicken coop. We left about a foot open all the way across the front of the lean-to roof so they'd have plenty of air. Tom built nesting boxes and put three roosting poles at different heights the full length of one side. It was good and tight to keep out night stalkers. Fifty baby chicks cost one dollar at the Mark Means Grainery in Lewiston. By the end of summer we'd have fryers, and by early fall the rest would be laying eggs. It seemed like the best investment. We handpicked our box of little, yellow fluff balls. They weren't quite old enough to tell whether they were hens or roosters. Roosters always start growing a comb first. "Peep, peep, peep," all the way home. What a contented sound they made. We put grass on the floor of the coop and filled the old feeder and watering jugs that Neen loaned us.

We had our first resident animals and were buying our own home. We were proud of what we had accomplished, but there was that ever-gnawing hole in the middle of life. The hole that could only be filled by a baby of our own.

On his way to work, Tom dropped me at the folks to pick berries around the middle of June. I went straight to the patch, knowing it was getting late in the day for picking. Where were they? I grabbed a *halic* and began picking. It wasn't even full before I heard an awful sound coming from the barn. "What in the world?" I ran to the barn. "Papa, Mama! Are you okay?" Opening the door, I saw, in the bright sunlight streaming in, Bossie standing, straining, and groaning. "What? You didn't tell me she was going to calve. What can I do to help?"

"Nothing really. Just waiting. Cows know what they're doing. It's hard on her 'cause it's her first time." Papa shook his head. "Sure wish we could help, but nature has to take her course."

Mama took me by the arm. "Come on, Susie. You and I'll go pick. Papa can handle this." So we picked, Bossie groaned, and I prayed for this young cow that all would go well.

It seemed like hours before we heard Papa yell, "Yippee! It's a boy." Mama smiled. "That means roast and steak." We finished picking our rows before we trudged to the barn. The full flats needed to be put in the shade.

Sure enough, there lay a little golden calf with its mama cleaning him up. I've always been amazed by the eyes of cattle—big, round, brown eyes with long lashes. When you stare into them, it seems they reflect the whole world. "You did well," Papa told Bossie as he petted her neck and side. "Good girl." She began to have spasms again. "She's just flushing the afterbirth." He announced. While Papa waited for the process, Mama and I went back to picking. Berries waited for no one, not even the wonder of birth.

The sun was high, must have been noon when we heard Papa calling from the barn. "Mama, Susie! Come quick." Fear filled both of us as we rushed to the barn. Papa turned with a grin as we opened the door. "Look here." He pointed to the hay. There lay another little calf with mother dutifully cleaning her precious second baby. "This one's a girl!" he announced. "Susie, here's your milk cow." She was tiny with the beautiful markings of a Jersey, and eyes twice as big as her brother's. They stared at me intently.

I started toward her, "Nope, stay back. Let Bossie take care of her. There'll be plenty of time for you two to get acquainted."

I looked at Papa. "Did you know it was going to be twins?"

"Nope, I think the good Lord did though. He planned one for us and an extra for you. Isn't He good?"

Mama shook her head. "She was already bred when we got her. Clyde said that was a bonus for being a good neighbor."

We finished picking while Papa cleaned up the barn—a second time. He changed his clothes and took the berries to town. I helped Mama get some supper ready. With all the calf excitement, we hadn't even thought of eating dinner. What a day!

Tom pulled in at eleven thirty that night, to take me home. I was wide awake, anticipating sharing with him the great baby news. I was almost as excited as if it had been my own child—well, maybe not that excited. I went out to the car. "Tom, do you have your flashlight in the car?"

"Of course, never without it."

"Get it and come with me." I ordered. "Now, promise me you'll be quiet," I whispered as we got closer to the barn.

"What's going . . ." I opened the door, took the flashlight from Tom's hand, and lit up the new babies and their mama. "Oh my golly!" was his response.

"Bossie had twins today," I beamed. "A boy and a girl. The girl is going to be our new milk cow." Tom stared at me. I thought maybe he didn't hear me. "Papa said the little girl will be ours." Then I noticed there were tears forming in Tom's eyes. I shut off the light.

"Your folks are so good to us. How can we ever repay them?" We walked slowly arm in arm to the car.

Chapter 59

Unexpected Cost

The future held chickens and a milk cow, but I had to think about food for now. The garden planted just east of the house was doing well. So far, we had harvested green beans, lettuce, and peas. It would take several weeks for other crops to develop. We couldn't live on greens alone. This took drastic measures. "I need to take ten dollars from savings to buy some food supplies," I told Tom after another evening meal of salad. "We can't survive on just salad."

The next day, we made a trip to the bank and stopped at the Safeway Store. I'd been told they had good prices. They happened to be having a sale on things I needed: a forty-nine-pound sack of flour for a dollar and thirty-nine cents, three pounds of salt for ten cents, three pounds of coffee for fifty cents, ten pounds of potatoes for twenty-five cents, five pounds of rolled oats for twenty cents, and four cans of meat for a dollar, for a total of three dollars and forty-four cents. The rest I tucked away for unexpected emergencies. Mama and Papa shared eggs with us until our chicks started laying. When their calves were weaned, they gave us their extra milk.

That emergency came sooner than expected. When Tom brought home his next check, he handed it to me with a long face. "The government's started taking out something called Social Security from my check. Said it's something for my old age. Man, don't they realize I need it now? I can't believe they're taking three dollars out every month. Just one month would buy ninety-eight pounds of flour—enough for a whole year of bread." It was what it was, and I couldn't think of anything to say. Tom put up the silent wall for the first time since we moved here. He was worried and didn't know how to handle it. Neither did I.

Toward the end of July, grain began ripening in Tammany, a flat area of farms spreading all the way from the Orchards to Waha Mountain. Tom drove a grain truck for the McIntosh family on his two days off. When that harvest was finished, he drove for the Howard Ranch down on Lindsey Creek. My man wasn't afraid of work. By the end of September, he put enough into savings to make up for the entire year of Social Security payments.

We discovered a small mill in the Orchards overlooking Tammany. It also had free mill-ends. We began filling the car and stacking wood against the back of the house. Thinking ahead is important to prepare for winter. We learned that lesson well on the Stick Ranch.

Three times that summer, we cut our six acres of grass with hand scythes, hauled it to the barn in an old wheelbarrow, and stacked it into the hayloft. I canned fruits and vegetables, and filled the shelves Tom had built in the kitchen. Two metal barrels held oats and chicken feed so the mice wouldn't get to it. Tom brought home buckets of grain spilled on the ground in the railroad yard from the shipping cars. It made good chicken feed or it could be cleaned, soaked, and used for cereal if we needed.

We celebrated Thanksgiving that year with our first chicken dinner. The hens were laying, but our little heifer, whom I named Elsie, wouldn't give milk until after she had her first calf. We left her at the folks so she could have the company of her mother and brother. Cows are social and like to be with their herd.

On December 31, we made our mortgage payment, paid the taxes and water bill, and still had a little in the savings account. We were so blessed.

Chapter 60

Home Improvement

Edna came home early one day when I was visiting the folks. "Look, look!" she bounced in the door and held out her left hand. "Luther asked me to marry him." Luther Moore had moved to the area to work on one of the big dams being built on the Columbia River.

"I'm so happy for you." I gave her a big hug. "What does he think of little Patty?" I still had in the back of my mind we could raise her.

"He adores her. He wants to raise her as his own daughter." She picked up Patty and gave her a hug. "We're so lucky." At last, maybe Edna could find a good life.

Tom and I had big plans for our home's second year.

We bred Elsie to the Martins' bull in December and brought her home. Cows have a nine-month gestation period just like people, so by the end of September, we'd have a calf and milk. She balked at going up the ramp into the back of Papa's little pickup, then panicked and jumped when the engine started. I climbed in with her, rubbed her face and neck, and talked to her the whole five miles. "It will be just fine, Elsie. We love you and will take good care of you. We've got a brand-new barn made just for you. You'll feel right at home. I'll come talk to you every day." She made it fine. I, on the other hand, was freezing.

I knew she'd miss her cow family. I made trips to the barn several times a day to scratch her neck and keep her company. Looking into her big, brown eyes and watching her ears perk up, I knew she was listening to every word. I told her everything. Guess you could say I used her for "cowplaining." I know, bad joke.

We wanted to add to our two rooms. We began in February at first thaw. For the first time in our building career, we dug ditches and made forms for the foundation. When it got warmer, we poured a concrete foundation ten feet toward the barn and all the way across the back of the house. We wanted it strong.

Tom dug a root cellar underneath the kitchen section of the house. He dug; I carried the buckets of dirt to the garden area and dumped them. At eight feet square and six feet high, the cellar held many shelves for storing home-canned goods. An old, brown ice chest sat on planks. Food wouldn't spoil in the hot summer when we could afford ice. A cellar is warmer in winter and cooler in summer. Stairs led down through a door on the floor of the new screened back porch. The other room, our bedroom, extended across the back of the house to the far wall. At last, we had a private bedroom.

The other house project? Real shingles on the entire roof before it started leaking. We were sold some gray asbestos, rolled roofing. "It's new," we were told. "The best there is. It will last a lifetime." Between these two projects, our savings was being eaten by the cost of materials.

In April, Tom burst in the door from work, yelling, "Susie, Susie! I got paid today."

"Uh-huh . . ." I knew it was payday. It was almost midnight. I rolled over.

He shined his flashlight on the check. It blinded me. When I focused, I couldn't believe what I saw. "Fifty dollars!"

"I got a raise, Susie. I've been there a year and they gave me a raise!" He grabbed me in a hug. "We've got to celebrate. Where's that grape juice you made last fall from the McMillanses' grapes?" He hurried out to the kitchen and started going through the cupboards. I crawled out of bed and got there in time for him to hand me a cup of juice. "To all the good things that are happening to us. How lucky we are!" We clinked our cups and drank.

I wanted to say, "Tom, it isn't luck. God's giving us these good things. He's heard my prayers." I knew any mention of God would ruin the moment and said, "Thank you," in my heart.

Chapter 61

Edna's Devastating News

Summer was a blur of planting, picking, canning, feeding critters, and mowing grass. Not a day went by that wasn't filled from sunup to sundown. June 30, 1938, the folks came with Edna and Patty. They brought a cake to celebrate my twenty-eighth birthday. On the Fourth of July, Tom and I drove to the Snake River to watch fireworks set off over the river. July 27, we went to the folks for dinner to celebrate Edna's twentieth birthday. Everyone was too busy in the summer to socialize much. Short bits of time were all that could be spared.

Two weeks after Edna's birthday celebration, Papa's old black pickup pulled into the driveway. Papa climbed out. I knew something was terribly wrong by his slumped shoulders and shuffling walk. I sat down my bucket of carrots and rushed over, wiping my dirty hands on my apron.

"I've got some bad news," he began, looking at the ground.

"Mama?" I asked.

He shook his head. "No, your sister." He looked up with tears in his eyes. "She got word by telephone this morning that Luther was killed in an accident at the dam."

I was dumbstruck. Here was a man who loved my sister, wanted to adopt Patty, and make a real family for the rest of their lives. How could God allow this to happen to my Edna? She wanted nothing more than to have life turn out all right. Papa and I held each other and cried.

"I need to go to Edna. Let me go change my apron and shoes." I hurried into the house then rode the five miles, wondering what I would say. Nothing I could offer would make any difference. It was what it was, and I could think of nothing to say. I could only help her cry.

Life did move on. Isn't it strange how the rest of the world keeps going when your world's brought to a screeching halt? Edna stumbled through, day after day, cooking and cleaning house for a family in downtown Lewiston. She was gone from Monday through Friday, coming home only on weekends. Tears were always near the surface, and she avoided people's sympathetic condolences. It worked best for her. Her daughter was her motivation. She often brought home a little wooden box of cheese for Patty to make up for being gone all week. Patty's general greeting at the door was, "Where's the cheese?" My heart ached for them, but I knew God had to do the healing.

Life moved on at our house, too. The new root cellar was filled with jars of fruit and vegetables, and Elsie gave birth to a little bull. Now we'd have fresh meat and our own milk. We built a pigpen and with plans to buy a pregnant sow. The Peiskelicks, on the corner of Twenty-First and Grelle, asked me to help pick their strawberries and fresh produce come summer to sell at their farmer's stand.

On Easter of '39, Edna brought home another fellow. His name was Helmuth, but everyone called him Pete because his last name was Peterson. He was a tall, gangly guy with a pleasant smile and a little chuckle. "Where do you hail from?" Papa asked.

"Well, I was born in Copenhagen, Denmark. Father was a guard at the palace. We came to the United States when I was eighteen months old. Father became a brick layer—a mason. He makes bricks and lays them for buildings at the University of Idaho." That was interesting. "He's bought farmland up on the Palouse."

It turned out Pete was the same age as me. I thought the five years between Tom and I was a big difference. Eight years? This didn't seem good. It didn't matter what I thought. Edna was desperate for security. Pete and Edna were married on July 15, 1939. They moved to a farm outside of Moscow where water came from a well, kerosene lamps gave light, food was cooked on a woodstove, and the fields were plowed by a team of horses. It was only a short step back in time.

What did matter were the differences between them. Edna loved people and socializing. Pete was happy to be a loner, except around family. Edna needed to be busy all the time. Pete was laid back and wanted to go fishing on the weekends. Outdoor allergies made life miserable for Edna. Pete was jealous and possessive. He had many strange ideas handed down from his folks' old-world culture. It was not a good match. Edna's free life was now caged.

Chapter 62

Snug as a Bug

Johnny and Alice lived six blocks from the folks. We seldom saw Johnny and never Alice. She refused to let him see his family. She consented to moving back to Lewiston when her mother became a widow. It was her duty as the older daughter to take care of her mother. All holidays were spent with Alice's family. Sometimes, Johnny would "slip off to run an errand" and stop by to visit a short time. For Mama, it seemed to be enough that Johnny lived in the same town.

The dynamics of my family changed. It was only the folks and us. We tried to visit them as often as time would let us. I knew they were lonely—especially without their granddaughter's constant energy filling the house. I helped Mama with canning and preparing for winter. Mama was a different person at sixty-seven. Her harsh tongue that used to lash me bitterly was stilled, and she often said, "I appreciate all you do, Susie." Hurts, sadness, and heartaches force us to look at others with new eyes.

Mama was peeling apples for applesauce while I was cutting them up in the big pot. "Susie, what will you do if you never have any kids?" I was taken back. Many people had asked about our lack of family, but never my mama. She had told me one time, "You're so lucky you don't have children. They only give you grief."

After a moment I replied, "I don't know. I decided not to think about it. There's nothing I can do, so I just keep on doing what I can do. If I'm s'posed to have a child, God will say 'yes,' and if I'm not,

God will say 'no.' I have to accept it and do the best I can with what He's given me."

"Hrmmph!" Mama threw a peeled apple in the pot. "God doesn't care a fig about you wanting a child. Look at me. I wanted boys, and what did I get? A pussyfooted, lazy boy and two girls. If we'd had boys, we'd still be on the farm. He didn't care what I wanted."

I had to think about that. The pot was full; I added sugar and some water and put it on the stove to cook. "I think God doesn't control everything in our lives. We make choices. He does the best He can with them. We have to choose to be happy where we are. Remember the stories you told about coming out West in the covered wagon? You were only eight but you always said, 'Doesn't do any use to complain. Things are the way they are.' It was a good way to look at hard times."

Mama was quiet. "Those days were impossible. How'd we survive?" She spread the apple peelings on the screen frames to dry. Good snacks in winter. "Yes, it didn't do any good to complain. Maybe I shoved so many complaints inside that I grew old and bitter. I'm no good for anyone now." I heard her sob as she hurried out the door to put the frames in the sun.

That show of Mama's emotions made me see life with clearer eyes. Her denial of early hardship brought a critical, judging attitude of anyone who wasn't stoic and strong. Life doesn't bend the way we want. It shifts and changes with events and choices. However, Mama's childhood philosophy was still a good one: "Doesn't do any use to complain. Things are the way they are." I would add, "Choose to be content wherever you find yourself."

The winter of '39–'40 was our first winter of contentment. Having been able to pay all our property debt and make huge improvements to our buildings, we were, as Tom would say, "snug as a bug in a rug."

We decided to put off buying a sow until April. Piglets would come in June or July. After six weeks, they'd be taken to the sales yard. Fall was a good time to sell both pigs and calves. Timing was important to get the best price. People were looking for their winter supply of meat. Of course, we'd keep one of the pigs for ourselves to smoke into hams and bacon. The beef, we'd have to keep in the ice chest in the cellar. We'd have meat next winter.

Neither Tom nor I were often sick. Why? I don't know. Maybe our hard work repelled all the germs. Maybe we didn't have time to admit we didn't feel good. In February of '40, Tom took a spell where he was throwing up a lot. It was so bad, he couldn't go to work. It was the first time I remember him being sick, other than a sore throat, in the almost twelve years we'd been married. He missed two days of work and spent his two days off in bed. "Got to get back to work," he huffed, as he fumbled with his work boots on the fifth day. "Can't afford to be sick any longer." Off he drove, white as a sheet, but managed to stay the whole day. As time went on, he got stronger.

The next week, it was my turn. It was horrible. I couldn't keep anything down. I began to wonder if some of our precious stored food might be spoiled. I ruled that out because we had eaten the same thing, but didn't get sick at the same time. Four days, five days . . . any time I even thought about food, my stomach churned. On the seventh day, I was able to eat a half slice of bread. It got a little better each day. We must have picked up a stomach bug someplace.

Chapter 63

YES!

The garden was planted and the sow was in the pen, spring had sprung. It was a time of waiting for things to grow. It was also a time of waiting for me. My female schedule seemed to be all off kilter. Nothing was right from the month we got sick. It was June before it occurred to me that maybe . . . just possibly . . . it could be . . . I was pregnant. I kept this secret to myself. What if I were wrong? I didn't want to get Tom's hopes up and have him disappointed. I'd play it safe, make sure before I said a single word.

The sow gave birth to eight little piglets in the middle of one July night. She had lain on one and smothered it before we found them in the morning. It was her first litter. I guess she had to learn to be a more cautious mother. She seemed to have enough milk. The babies were adorable. All babies are, you know.

One was especially small. "I think we should keep the runt," Tom said as he checked how many females there were. They'd bring more money because they could be bred. "If we always keep the runt for ourselves, we'll make more money selling the others." It sounded like a good plan to me. I stood amazed again at the wonder of birth. What a great plan, God! Was this happening to me? I held tight to my secret.

By the middle of August, I knew my secret was a reality. I was going to have Tom's baby —our baby. I would tell him on his next day off. I wanted to cook a special dinner to make my announcement. First, I'd make a trip to town. A bus service began running along Grelle to downtown Lewiston twice a day two years ago. I sometimes took it to the folks during berry picking because it ran just a block from their house and returned in late afternoon. "I'm going to take the bus this morning." I looked at Tom across the breakfast table. "I'd like to visit the folks." It was not quite a lie, but close. At the cost of twenty cents on a round trip, I could do this a couple times a month. He never begrudged me going to visit them.

Except, today I wasn't going to the folks. I was going to see Dr. Carsow, the railroad doctor. I'd never been to a doctor, unless you could count the yellow jaundice episode when the doctor came to our house.

The doctor's office was on the second floor of a building at the corner of Ninth and Main. The woman behind the desk looked at me and smiled, "Good morning. What can we do for you today?"

"My husband works for Camas Prairie Railroad. I was told Dr. Carsow is the railroad doctor." I was very nervous.

"That's right. All railroad employees and their families get to see the doctor free of charge." She smiled again.

"Good. I'd like to see him." I turned to walk through the door that said Doctor Carsow.

"Wait," the lady jumped up from behind the desk blocking me from the door. "Uh, first we need you to fill out some paperwork." She sat back down. "Now, what's your name?"

"Susan Chase." I felt my resolve melting and my knees getting week.

"Husband's name?"

"Thomas Albert Chase."

"Your address?"

"My mailing or street address?"

"Both please." She glanced up. I was sure she thought I was from the far reaches of civilization.

"Route 2 Box 366 is our mailbox. We live at 2023 Grelle in the Lewiston Orchards."

She continued asking question after question. Then she got very personal. "And what's the reason for your visit today?"

I didn't think that was any of her business. That was the reason I wanted to see the doctor. "Why do you need to know?"

"It needs to be recorded so the railroad will know your reason for seeing the doctor. They'll be the one paying for your visit."

"I see. I'm having some female problems." I couldn't bring myself to tell a complete stranger the most wonderful news of my life, before I even told my husband.

"All right, Mrs. Chase. Have a seat and I'll see if the doctor's busy." She disappeared in the door and I collapsed into a chair.

I hadn't even warmed the seat before she opened the door and invited me in. It was a sparse room. A small brown desk piled high with papers stood in the far corner, and a long, brown, wooden table was in the middle of the floor. There was one chair by the wall and a high-backed chair on wheels behind the desk. "Please have a seat, Susan."

Somehow, I expected a more professional approach. He did have on a white shirt and brown slacks, but no tie. All the windows were open and yet the room was stifling, almost as much as our poorly ventilated house. His light brown hair was long on top but short on the sides. He wore small, gold, wire-rimmed glasses. The only clue that he was a doctor was the thing he wore around his neck. He pulled out a glass stick from his desk and said, "Open up. Put this under your tongue. Yes, close." Then he started asking questions. I could only answer by nodding or shaking my head. At last, he asked, "Are you pregnant, Susan?" I nodded.

He took thermometer out of my mouth and directed me to lie down on the table. He poked around my stomach for a bit, smiled and said, "Yes, you are. It will probably come about the end of October or first of November." He went to his desk and wrote his phone number on a small piece of paper and handed it to me. "Give me a call when you go into labor and I'll come deliver it." He walked over, opened the door, and showed me out.

Is that all? I wanted to yell. *You're not giving me any directions, advice, or warnings?* As usual, I kept my yelling tucked safely in my mind where it wouldn't cause a problem. I left quietly. By the time I reached the street, I was too excited to care. I hurried to the five-and-dime store in the next block and bought a small bib. We were going to have a baby!

Chapter 64

The Announcement

I had only one day to plan my surprise. I carefully wrote "Baby Chase" with a pencil on the white bib. I dug through the embroidery floss trying to decide what color to use. Blue, since that was always what he hoped for, boys. I don't know where that color thing for boys and girls came from. It wouldn't matter. Blue was Tom's favorite color.

I kept my conversation short during breakfast the next morning. I was about to explode with the news and couldn't trust my mouth not to blurt it out and spoil everything. I would embroider the bib and write a poem to read before giving it to him at supper.

We got up about the same time. Even on Tom's days off, animals had to be fed and watered, and there were always weeds to hoe and watering to do before it got too hot. I joined Tom in the garden, picking corn for dinner and digging carrots, an onion, and some early potatoes to throw in with the roast. The peaches were ripening. We'd have fresh peaches with cream from the top of the morning milk.

I built a good-sized fire, put biscuits to raise, and a beef roast in the oven while Tom was out moving the sprinklers on the newly planted patch of alfalfa. "I'm gonna walk down and talk to Pa Daniels. See about borrowing his tractor to cut the grass," he called through the screen door.

"Okay." I called back. Good. That would give me time to get things done. Maybe even get me off my feet a little. I found I needed to rest more. Visits with Pa Daniels were always good for at least two hours.

Two and a half hours later, I heard Tom wash up in the bucket on the back porch and comb his hair in the old mirror hanging above it, like he always did before supper. Must have been something his mother expected of her kids. When he came in the kitchen, he whistled, "Smells good in here. What's the occasion? It's not our anniversary yet, is it?"

I laughed, "No, just celebrating your day off."

When we were seated, I looked at my impressively strong man and knew I couldn't wait until after supper. "Don't," I said, as he reached to stab some meat with his fork. "I've got something to read first." He slowly put down the fork and I read:

> We've worked hard to get this far.
> The railroad lets you fix boxcars.
> Our land's producing all we need,
> Vegetables, fruit and our cow's feed.
> We've got chicks, a calf and pigs.
> We need to throw a big shindig
> 'Cause don't you think that just—just maybe
> It's time we have our own little baby?

I handed him the little bib rolled and tied with a ribbon. He stared at it and me, slowly unrolling it. "Baby Chase!" he yelled. "We're gonna have a baby?" I'm sure Ma and Pa Daniels could hear him a half block away.

I nodded. He jumped around the table and grabbed me in a tight squeeze. "Uh, Tom." I was gasping for air.

He let go with a start, "I'm sorry, did I hurt you? Did I hurt the baby? Is this really happening?" He ran out the backdoor yelling, "Hey, Elsie! We're gonna have a baby! Hens, we're gonna have a baby! You old sow, we're gonna have a baby too!"

Chapter 65

Baby Chase

It was the middle of September before we told anyone else. By that time, even if the baby came early, it would be healthy. Papa was thrilled. Mama was upset. "Why'd you wait so long to tell us? How do you expect me to get anything made in such a short time? The old sewing machine's been acting up. Something's wrong with the treadle timing. I'll have to make something by hand . . .," she went on and on.

"It's okay, Mama." I assured her. "We just wanted to make sure."

"It's not a good time to bring a baby into a world with war brewing all over. Who knows what's going to happen? Hope it's a girl." I was enveloped in my own ecstasy, oblivious to the war that had been going for about 14 months. It was far off physically and mentally. How could it affect us? My mother was a negative reactor. However, she was smiling and congratulating us before we left, excited to be a grandma again at almost sixty-eight.

Edna was delighted to think Patty would have a little cousin to play with. She promised to get to Lewiston as often as possible so they would be good friends. We stopped by Johnny and Alice's house to share the news. Alice's piercing angry eyes and mean, untempered mouth let us know we weren't welcome. We left. Oh dear. We had done to them what so many had done to us in the last twelve years. We were too excited to think clearly. A couple of weeks later, I received a letter from her. I was pleased, thinking it was an apology. It was full of angry words and accusations about Mama. "Don't you dare let your mother be around your baby. She'll ruin it for life, just like she's ruined our lives." I understood the jealousy and resentment that consumed her. I felt sorry for her. My heart was even heavier for my brother who was trapped in a house of anger and bitterness. I couldn't keep from wondering how different his life would have been if he'd married Tom's sister, Frankie.

Neen gathered all the Chase family at her house for a dinner on Sunday afternoon. Tom's father didn't come. He was too ill. Was that a fact or was he avoiding us? Tom hadn't seen his father since he packed him up and took him away from the river.

Of course, the family was elated. Paris' little boy, Clifford LeRoy, was the cutest, black-haired, blue-eyed boy you ever saw. He was ten months old. Everyone knew these two babies would be close cousins. This would be the fifteenth Chase grandchild. The oldest was eighteen. Mother Chase was beaming.

Two weeks later, Tom came home early from work and found me lying on the bed. "You all right?" There was deep concern in his voice.

"I think so. The pigs rooted a hole under the fence and three escaped the pen. I had a hard time getting them rounded up. Haven't run so much in ages. All this extra baby weight slows me down."

Tom scowled. "That does it. I'll get Saturday off and take them to the auction. Can't have my baby coming out lookin' like a pig because its mother was chasing 'em." I must have looked at him strange. "Haven't you heard? Things like that mark babies. Sometimes, they'll even get birthmarks from things happening beforehand."

"Oh, Tom. That's old wives' tales," I chided. I'd not realized the Chase family was extremely superstitious. Black cats crossing your path, bad luck. Drop a knife, a man's coming to dinner; a fork, a woman's coming; a spoon, a child's coming. If you run out of kerosene, you'll be in the dark for thirty days. Meaning, you won't know what's going on. The list was long.

Tom stuck to his plan and took the pigs to market. He came home again jiggity-jig with a hundred and forty-four dollars. It had been a profitable investment. He patched the hole in the fence so the little runt couldn't escape.

Chapter 66

It Happened with a Bang

Around 4 a.m. on Thursday, November 7, 1940, I woke with a start. *What's that?* . . . I drifted back to sleep. The pains have started. Immediately, my mind flew back to my eighth year when Mama was giving birth to Edna. I remembered the screams, the smells, the worried looks. Would it be that way with me? Not even Mama or Edna would explain anything to me. No one talked about things like that. It was hush-hush and private. It would be what it would be.

It so happened, it was Tom's day off work. *Thank you, God.* He wouldn't have to miss a day of work. He began to stir about six-thirty. He got up to stoke the fire and warm up the house. "Sweetie, how early do you think the Yarbers get up?" I questioned. They were the only neighbors in a mile that had a phone.

"Oh, I 'spect Grandpa Yarber gets up pretty early. He's got two cows ta milk. Why?" All older people in that day were called Grandpa and Grandma. This special couple had befriended and helped us when we first moved into the neighborhood.

"I'm thinking maybe you should go ask if you can use their phone to call Doctor Carsow."

"What? Where's that paper? I know I laid that phone number right . . . right there on the top. . ." Tom panicked and clawed through the papers piled on our dresser.

"Calm down. It's not time yet. I just want him to know so he can plan the day." I lay back on the pillow and chuckled at my husband.

"While you're at it, go up to Mattoon's and get Myrtle. Remember, she said she'd come be our nurse since she works at the hospital."

"All right, all right." Tom was throwing clothes on. He grabbed his coat and left, forgetting to close the door behind him. His fire would do no good with the door wide open. I got up, closed it, and returned to the bedroom. Not much heat got back to that room. I crawled down deep into the still warm quilts.

I woke twice to pains while Tom was gone. In between, I was having wonderful dreams about bridges. When the door opened, the alarm clock said seven-thirty. Tom had brought Myrtle with him. "She'll know what to do until the doctor gets here," he said to comfort me. Myrtle started filling me in on what to expect. Tom didn't want to hear and left out the backdoor. I could hear him chopping wood while we talked.

"That will keep him busy," she laughed. "It's always the husband who gets in the way." Her calmness helped me relax, and I knew it would go well.

At eight-thirty, Doc Carsow arrived—with pistol in hand. Oh my, this was not reassuring. "Hope you don't mind if I do some target practice in your backyard." It was a statement, not a question. What could I say? He checked me and stated flatly: "It'll be a while. Myrtle, let me know when the contractions are a minute apart." She nodded.

Minutes later, I heard him discussing with Tom where to put the target so it wouldn't cause damage. What an odd doctor.

There wasn't much rest in the next three hours. It was either pains or gunshots pulling me out of half sleep. Myrtle brought a rubber sheet and put it under me. It was hot and sticky and moved with me every time I tried to find a place to get comfortable.

Bang, bang, bang . . . quiet . . . sleep . . . pain . . . sleep . . . bang, bang, bang . . . quiet . . .

The pains grew closer together. "That's good." Myrtle opened the back screen door and called the doctor. The shooting stopped, and I heard him stomping mud off his feet on the porch.

"Are you ready?" he asked her.

"Yes, clean clothes, warm water, towels—we're ready."

He washed his hands in the bucket and came into the small, one-windowed room.

"It would help to have some light. Do you have a flashlight so we don't have to light the lantern?" I nodded, and Myrtle hurried to ask Tom.

Suddenly, the pains changed and I knew it was time. Doctor nodded and said, "Push, breathe . . . now push." The pattern became more intense along with the pain until I barely had time to breathe. Suddenly, I felt the baby slip from my body into the world. The wonder of birth returned. How amazing it is! Our little girl began to cry as Myrtle cleaned her. It was beautiful music.

Doc Carsow turned his attention back to me, washed his hands, packed his medical kit, his gun and target, and said, "Congratulations," and was gone. You might say our baby literally came into the world with a "bang."

Myrtle placed our daughter beside me and fetched Tom.

This is the bridge I've longed to be—the bridge between generations, spanning not just changes, inventions, and experiences, but living relationships. This bridge named Susan had learned endurance, patience, trust, obedience, faith, and love. This child I just gave birth to will walk her own life bridge into the future. My heart sang with contentment. My life's complete and perfect.

Printed in the United States
By Bookmasters